Patterns for
North Ronaldsay
(and other 4 ply/fingering and aran weight)
Yarns

Elizabeth Lovick
Elly Doyle

Page Design
Elizabeth Lovick

Technical Editor
Elly Doyle

Photography
Elizabeth Lovick, Natasha Stacey

Cover
Judith Brodnicki

Northern Lace Press

Flotta — Orkney — Scotland

Patterns for North Ronaldsay
(and other 4 ply/fingering and aran weight)
Yarns

copyright Elizabeth Lovick 2017
Published by
Northern Lace Press
Braevalla, Weyland Bay
Kirkwall
Orkney, KW15 1TD

ISBN 978-0-9930614-8-6

Northern Lace Press

Flotta — Orkney — Scotland
www.northernlacepress.co.uk

Introduction

I started designing for North Ronaldsay wool as soon as I moved to Orkney in 1995. Blanster was produced later that year, and the original sweater is still in use, with the only sign of its age a coffee stain on the front! Other designs followed during the next couple of years, and the first edition of this book was produced in about 1997.

The world of knitting has changed dramatically in the past 20 years. The rise of the internet brought the ability to see and buy so many more yarns from so many more countries. Twenty years ago it was daring to buy from other continents; now we do it all the time. What we expect from a pattern has changed. No longer is it acceptable to say "work the second side to match", and patterns need to be in a wider range of sizes. I decided it was time to bring out a new, enlarged and updated edition.

Over the years, styles of photography have changed, as have the styles of glasses! But I have kept in some of the original photos, either for amusement value or because the original item has been given away. New photographs have been taken on various islands including North Ronaldsay itself, South Ronaldsay, Flotta and in Kirkwall, Orkney's county town.

As Elly Doyle has taken over from me dyeing the North Ronaldsay yarn, I invited her to add some of her patterns to the mix. Elly has also done the technical editing on the patterns and has acted as model for some of the garments. Natasha Stacey has modeled other garments, taken some of the photos and has been responsible for the accuracy of the page design. Both have also been invaluable sounding boards during the production of the book. Judith Brodnicki has again produced a wonderful cover for the book, and I am grateful for her skills and advice.

As the North Ronaldsay is such a rare breed, the amount of yarn produced each year is small. But these patterns can be used for many other yarns of the same thickness, and suggestions are given at the back of the book. Most of the patterns can also be varied and so there is also a section giving suggestions of what might be possible. I always like to think of my patterns as a starting point, and love it when people devise their own individual take on a garment.

I hope you enjoy both looking at, and working, from this book.
May it bring a little bit of the magic of Orkney with it!

Elizabeth Lovick
Orkney 2017

Sheep outside the dyke on the northern shores of North Ronaldsay.
The harsh conditions lead to a soft yarn.

Contents

North Ronaldsay Sheep 6
North Ronaldsay Yarn 8
Caring for Your Pieces 10

THE PATTERNS

Triangular Shawl 12
Garter Rib Collar 14
Betty Martin Cowl 15
Mistake Rib Beanie 16
Fingerless Mittens 18
Switha Cushion 20
Flotta Cushion 22
Cat's Paw Wrap 24
Simple Lacy Sweaters 26
Lacy Scarves 28
Lacy Cowls 30
Lacy Cushion Covers 32
Cat's Paw Stripe Scarf 35
Sampler Throw 36
Stocking Stitch Top 42
End-to-End Crescent 45
Beret and Fingerless Mittens 50
Roving Bags 52
V-Necked Vest 54
Braeland Sweater 58
Quoyeden Sweater 60
Blanster Sweater 64
Braeland Hat 68
Quoyeden Hat 70
Blanster Hat 72
Braeland Mittens 74
Quoyeden and Blanster Mittens 76
Braeland, Quoyeden and Blanster Scarves ...78
Cat's Paw Cropped Top 80
Cabled Scarf 82
Child's Vest 84
Striped Triangular Shawl (ED) 86
Skinny Crescent Shawl (ED) 88
Flouer Shawl (ED) 91
Child's Shawl-Necked Sweater (ED) 95

TECHNIQUES

Making Tassels 99
Making Pompoms 99
Preparing Roving for Knitting 100
Lining a Bag 100
Felting a Bag 100
Knitting i-cord 100

VARIATIONS

Measurements and Sizing 101
Using Other Yarns 102
Pattern Variations 103
Patterns by Type and Yarn Weight 107

PATTERN NOTES

Notes 108
General Abbreviations 108
Working from a Chart 108
Chart Symbols 109
Knitting Abbreviations 109

Index 110

North Ronaldsay Sheep

On the rocks and beaches of the tiny island of North Ronaldsay live herds of rare breed sheep. Their diet of seaweed and the harsh weather conditions produce a fleece which is warm and thick, with a long staple.

No one knows exactly how and when sheep came to North Ronaldsay. Excavations at the Broch of Burrian on the south-east tip of the island uncovered many spindle whorls and weaving combs, indicating a thriving wool-based industry two thousand years ago. DNA tests show that these Iron Age sheep are genetically identical to the modern sheep, showing that they have remained unchanged.

North Ronaldsays are a primitive breed, genetically the most primitive in the UK. Unlike most sheep, they have a double coat, the inner being as fine as cashmere and the outer being thicker. The outer coat, or guard hair, is structured to encourage water to run off the hair rather than soak into the undercoat.

In the Nineteenth Century, a wall was built round the island to confine the sheep to the shore, leaving the good grazing land for cattle. The sheep changed their biology and behaviour to adapt to live on the seaweed brought in by the tide. They can be seen on the rocks and sandy beaches eating fronds of their favourite laminaria like spaghetti.

North Ronaldsays do not appreciate fences and walls - these are there to be jumped or climbed. The dyke round the island is 5 or 6 feet high in most places - anything less is no obstacle to them. They are extremely sure-footed and agile and can race across slippery rocks at an amazing speed.

North Ronaldsay Yarn

Jane Donnelly, born and bred on the island, is the manager of the company 'A Yarn from North Ronaldsay' which produces rovings and yarn on a Canadian Mini-Mill. The total island clip is about three and a half tons of raw fleece, of which Jane has about two to two and a half tons.

The process begins when Jane selects about three times the weight of fleece for the amount of yarn required. This is washed in a large commercial washing machine, saving and reusing water to conserve energy. The washed fleece is then dried on on racks and left until needed.

Once dry, the fleece is opened up by an automated picker, teasing the matted bits apart and finally blowing it into a purpose-built room. The fibre is now passed through the de-hairer, a vital stage to produce a soft yarn, which removes the heavier guard hairs by centrifugal force. Typically, the first pass removes about a quarter of the mass. Different colour fleeces contain differing amounts of the guard hairs and the grey fibre may need a second pass through the de-hairer.

Next comes carding, producing roving, which may be sold to hand spinners, or processed further into yarn. The fibre is pulled over a series of drums giving a rope of fibre ready to spin.

Once the singles are spun they are plied. For the aran weight yarn, three singles are used and for the 4 ply/ fingering yarn, two.

When the wool is processed, some of the grease is left in the yarn giving it a stringy feel. However, when it is washed, the grease dissolves and the fibres relax, giving a fabric which is soft, light and warm.

Spinning the roving into singles is the most demanding of all the processes, and it requires skill to control. The threads produced are fine and can easily break. If the rovings are too oily, too wet or too dry they will not spin well.

North Ronaldsay wool dyes very well, either as the roving or the yarn. Elly Doyle, the Prim Peacock, dyes the yarn to sell in Orkney and online. As this yarn has already been washed, it feels much softer than the natural yarn.

Caring for your North Ronaldsay Pieces

With a bit of care, your knitted item will last for many years. The original Blanster *(below right)* is now over 20 years old! After you have worn your garment turn it inside out and put it over the back of a chair over night to let the smells of the day evaporate. Then fold it and put it away. If storing over the summer, fold it neatly and place in an old pillow case with cedar cubes or lavender to deter moths.

Unlike synthetic yarns, wool shrugs off dirt and smells. This means that a woollen garment does not have to be washed as often as a synthetic one. For all wool pieces, wipe spills as soon as they happen. Liquid tends to stay on the surface of the wool, so sponging will usually remove most stains. Be careful not to rub as this will roughen the yarn and may show.

WASHING A NORTH RONALDSAY PIECE

Sheep live in the rain, so water does not harm wool. However, the molecules that make up the wool fibres are helical and so can stretch if hung full of water.

HEAVY GARMENTS

Use either a specialist wool liquid or a good quality washing-up liquid (dish soap). Fill a large bowl or sink with hand hot water, and add the liquid to make a good lather. If the garment is big, and you only have a small bowl it is better to use the bath (or to dry clean). Drop the garment in and swish it about. Squeeze it, but do not rub or wring it. Lift it out, squeezing as much water out of it as possible, as the weight of the water can cause the garment to stretch if you are not careful. Rinse in a bowl of hand hot water, and repeat the rinsing with another bowl of water, adding a wool-specific fabric conditioner to the final rinse. Now put the garment in a wash bag or pillow case, and give it a wool cycle spin in your washing machine (600 to 900 rpm). If a washing machine is not available, lay the garment on a towel, and roll the towel up to form a Swiss roll with the garment as the filling. Now squeeze the roll to remove as much water as possible from the garment. Repeat with two or three more towels. Ideally lay the garment flat to let it dry, or place it on a woolly board.

DO NOT hang it by the shoulders or hem. If necessary, place it over a rail under the arms. Do not iron as this will flatten any pattern. Instead, shake the garment periodically during the drying, and pull in to shape.

LACE AND FINE WOOL GARMENTS

Use either a specialist wool liquid or a good quality washing-up liquid (dish soap). Fill a bowl with hand-hot water, and add the liquid to make a good lather. Drop the garment in and swish it about. Squeeze it, but do not rub or wring it.

Lift it out and squeeze as much water out of it as possible. Rinse in a bowl of hand hot water, and repeat the rinsing with another bowl of water. Now put the garment in a washing bag or pillow case, and give it a wool cycle spin in your washing machine (between 600 and 900 rpm).

If a washing machine is not available, lay the garment on a towel, and roll the towel up to form a 'Swiss roll' with the garment as the filling. Squeeze the roll to remove as much water as possible. Lay the piece flat to let it dry, pinning out lace to shape. If necessary, iron the piece on the wrong side with a cool iron and leave in the airing cupboard to dry completely.

DRESSING OR BLOCKING

This is the process of drying lace under tension. By stretching the piece, the holes open up and the true beauty of the lace is revealed.

Ideally this process requires dressing wires, pins and blocking mats. If these are not available one or more fluffy towels will work almost as well. A flat surface is also needed where the piece can be left to dry naturally.

Your piece should be washed as described above. Once it has been spun, shake it out and lay it on the board or towels. Starting from the centre, smooth the piece out. If using wires, thread these through a suitable line of holes. Now start to stretch the lace into shape, pinning the wires in place, and pinning out each scallop on any borders. You will probably find that the first pins have to be replaced later.

Once the piece is taut and the correct shape, leave it to dry thoroughly before removing the pins.

If you do not have wires, place the piece on top of fluffy towels on a flat surface. Smooth the lace outwards and pin any scallops in place. The friction between the wool and the pile of the towels will keep the item stretched out.

Warning: As with all knitted lace, your piece will look scraggy until it is washed and stretched or ironed. Have faith!!

SWATCHING

If you want a garment to fit you MUST swatch first. If you do not, you may find your garment is too big or too small.

Knit up a piece at least 6" wide using the stitch pattern over which the tension is to be measured. When you have knitted at least 6", cast off, then wash and block your work (p10). Once dry, unpin the swatch and count the number of stitches and rows to 4". If your numbers per 4" are below the given tension, use a size smaller needle; if they are above the given tension, use a size bigger needle.

Note that with the natural coloured yarn it is essential to measure the tension after the swatch has been thoroughly washed, as the yarn will bloom considerably.

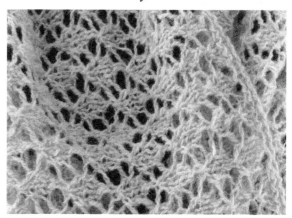

Triangular Shawl

Light and warm, this simple shawl is characteristic of Orkney design: it is simple and effective. It knits up quickly, and can be worn in many ways.

The shawl uses Cat's Paw and Old Shale on a garter stitch ground. The centre is knitted first, stitches are picked up along the row ends and the border is knitted outwards. Finally a small border is knitted along the top edge.

MATERIALS

100g North Ronaldsay fine yarn
pair 6 mm (US 10) needles
stitch markers

SIZE

48" wide and 28" deep

TENSION

13 sts and 21 rows to 4" over pattern after washing and blocking

PATTERN

CENTRE

Cast on 11 sts.
Work the 8 rows of the Tip Chart. 19 sts
Now work the 8 rows of the Centre Chart seventeen times, finishing after an 8th row. 155 sts
Do not break yarn. Leave sts on a thread.

BORDER

Pick up and knit 72 sts down to the cast on edge, PM. Pick up 11 sts from the cast on edge and work them a follows:

kfb 4 times, k4, kfb 3 times, PM. Pick up and knit 72 sts from the tip to the top. 162 sts

Increase Row: [K1, yo, k1] to M, RM, k to M, RM, [K1, yo, k1] to end of row. 234 sts.

Work through the Border Chart three times, then knit 1 row.

Cast off loosely, but do not break yarn.

TOP EDGE

With RSF, pick up and knit 10 sts from the edge of the border, knit the 155 sts held from the centre, then pick up and knit 10 from the edge of the border. 175 sts

Next Row: S1p, k to end of row. Repeat this row three times more. Cast off loosely.

FINISHING

Weave in ends. Wash and block, pulling the lace into smooth scallops.

CHARTS

TIP CHART

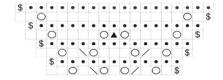

Row 1: S1p, k1, yo, k1, k2tog, yo, k1, yo, ssk, k1, yo, k2.
Row 2 and all even numbered rows: S1p, k to end of row.
Row 3: S1p, k1, yo, k1, k2tog, yo, k3, yo, ssk, k1, yo, k2.
Row 5: S1p, k1, yo, k4, yo, k3togtbl, yo, k4, yo, k2.

Row 7: S1p, k1, yo, k to last 2 sts, yo, k2.
Row 8: S1p, k to end of row.

CENTRE CHART

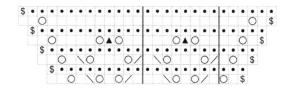

Row 1: S1p, k1, yo, *k1, k2tog, yo, k1, yo, ssk, k2. Repeat from * to last 9 sts, k1, k2tog, yo, k1, yo, ssk, k1, yo, k2.
Row 2 and all even numbered rows: S1p, k to end of row.
Row 3: S1p, k1, yo, k1, *k2tog, yo, k3, yo, ssk, k1. Repeat from * to last 2 sts, yo, k2.
Row 5: S1p, k1, yo, k2, *k2, yo, k3togtbl, yo, k3. Repeat from * to last 3 sts, k1, yo, k2.
Row 7: S1p, k1, yo, k to last 2 sts, yo, k2.
Row 8: S1p, k to end of row.

BORDER CHART

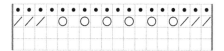

Row 1: K.
Row 2: P.
Row 3: *K2tog three times, [yo, k1] six times, k2tog three times. Repeat from * to end of row.
Row 4: K.

Garter Rib Collar

A very simple, warm and stylish alternative to a scarf. In Orkney it has the advantage of not blowing away! If you prefer, hold the two ends together with a brooch rather than a button. In wear fold the back of the collar over so that it snuggles against the neck.

MATERIALS

90 (100, 115, 130) g aran weight yarn
pair 4.5 mm (US 8) needles
One large button

SIZES

To fit: child (teen, woman, plus)
Width: 5 (6, 7, 8)"
Length: 22 (26, 30, 34)"
Length easily adjustable.

TENSION

18 st and 28 rows to 4" over pattern

PATTERN

Cast on 24 (28, 32, 36) sts.

Rows 1 and 2: S1p, k to end of row.

Rows 3 and 4: S1p, (k1, p1) to last st, k1.

These 4 rows form the pattern. Work 14 (18, 22, 26) rows more in pattern.

Next Row: S1p, patt 9 (11, 13, 15), k2tog, yo, yo, yo, k3togtbl, patt to end of row.

Next Row: S1p, patt 11 (13, 15, 17), p1 (into second yo), patt to end of row.

Staring with Row 3, work in pattern until the collar measures 22 (26, 30, 34)" from the start, finishing after Row 1.

Adjust length here. Cast off.

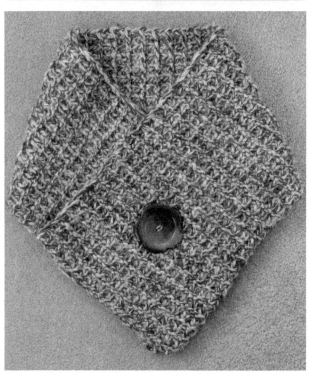

FINISHING

Weave in ends. Fold as shown in the photo, and sew the button in place.

Betty Martin Cowl

This cowl uses a simple stitch pattern which has the advantage of being as attractive on the 'wrong' side as on the 'right' side. The stitch pattern is often used in fishermen's ganseys, and is know as Betty Martin. No one knows why...

MATERIALS

55 (60, 70, 80, 95) g aran weight yarn

5 mm (US 8) circular needle

SIZES

To fit: child (teen, woman, plus)

Width: 7 (8, 9, 10)"

Circumference: 17 (19, 21, 23)"

Width easily adjustable.

TENSION

17 st and 28 rows to 4" over pattern after washing and blocking

PATTERN

Cast on 72 (80, 92, 100) sts and join to work in the round.

Rnds 1 and 2: *K2, p2. Repeat from * to end of rnd.

Rnds 3 and 4: K.

These 4 rounds form the pattern.

Repeat them until the work measures 7 (8, 9, 10)", ending after a 2nd round. Adjust length here.

Cast off.

FINISHING

Weave in ends.

Mistake Rib Beanie

Everyone in the family will wear this beanie - old, young, male, female. The fabric is very stretchy, so it will not blow off, and will accommodate growing heads.

MATERIALS

50 (55, 60, 70, 80) g aran weight yarn
pairs 4.5 and 5 mm (US 7 and 8)
needles

SIZES

To fit: toddler (child, teen, woman, man)
Head circumference: 16 (18, 20, 22, 24)"
Note - the stitch pattern is very stretchy.

TENSION

16 st and 24 rows to 4" in pattern on larger needles when slightly stretched

PATTERN

With 4.5 mm needles, cast on 66 (74, 82, 90, 98) sts and work 4 (4, 6, 6, 6) rows in k1, p1 rib.
Next Row: kfb, rib to end of row. 67 (75, 83, 91, 99) sts

Change to 5 mm needle.
Row 1: *K2, p2. Repeat from * to last 3 sts, k2, p1.
Repeat this row for 3 (4, 5, 6, 7)".

Shape top:
Row 1: K1, * k1, p2, k2, p1, k2tog. Repeat from * to last 2 sts, k1, p1.
Row 2: K2, *p1, k2, p2, k2. Repeat from * to last st, p1.
Row 3: K1, *k1, p2, k2, k2tog. Repeat from * to last 2 sts, k1, p1.
Row 4: K2, *p1, k1, p2, k2. Repeat from * to last st, p1.
Row 5: K1, *k1, p2, k1, k2tog. Repeat from * to last 2 sts, k1, p1.
Row 6: K2, *p3, k2. Repeat from * to last 2 sts, p1.
Row 7: K1, *k1, p2, k2tog. Repeat from * to last 2 sts, k1, p1.
Row 8: K2, *p2tog, k2. Repeat from * to last st, p1.
Row 9: K1, *k1, k2tog. Repeat from * to last 2 sts, k1, p1.
Row 10: P2tog across row.
Row 11: K2tog across row, working an odd st at the end of the row as k1.
Break yarn and draw through remaining sts.

FINISHING

Sew back seam. Weave in ends.
Wash and dry flat.

Fingerless Mittens

Simple enough for a child or beginner to make, these mitts match the Garter Rib Collar (p14), the Betty Martin Cowl (p15) and the Mistake Ribbing Beanie (p16) The mitts are very simple, with no shaping. The stretchy fabric will hug your hands leaving your fingers free.

FOR EACH PAIR OF MITTS

MATERIALS
40 (45, 50, 60, 70) g aran weight yarn
pairs 4.5 and 5 mm (US 7 and 8) needles

SIZES
To fit: toddler (child, teen, woman, plus, man)
Palm circumference: 5 (6, 7, 8, 9, 10)"
Note - all the stitch patterns are stretchy

TENSION
16 st and 24 rows to 4" in pattern on larger needles when slightly stretched

Betty Martin Mitts

With 4.5 mm needles, cast on 22 (26, 30, 34, 38, 42) sts and work 8 (10, 12, 14, 16, 18) rows in k1, p1 rib.

Change to 5 mm needle.
Row 1: K.
Row 2: P.
Row 3: K2, *p2, k2. Repeat from * to end of row.
Row 4: P2, *k2, p2. Repeat from * to end of row.
Repeat these 4 rows until the mitt measures 4 (5, 6, 7, 8, 9)" from the start.
Cast off in pattern.

Garter Rib Mitts

With 4.5 mm needles, cast on 22 (26, 30, 34, 38, 42) sts and work 8 (10, 12, 14, 16, 18) rows in k1, p1 rib.

Change to 5 mm needle.
Rows 1 and 2: S1p, k to end of row.
Rows 3 and 4: S1p, (k1, p1) to last st, k1.
Repeat these 4 rows until the mitt measures 4 (5, 6, 7, 8, 9)" from the start.
Cast off in pattern.

Mistake Rib Mitts

With 4.5 mm needles, cast on 22 (26, 30, 34, 38, 42) sts and work 8 (10, 12, 14, 16, 18) rows in k1, p1 rib.
Next Row: Kfb, rib to end of row. 23 (27, 31, 35, 39, 43) sts

Change to 5 mm needle.
Row 1: *K2, p2. Repeat from * to last 3 sts, k2, p1.
Repeat this row until the mitt measures 4 (5, 6, 7, 8, 9)" from the start.
Cast off in pattern.

FINISHING (ALL MITTS)
Sew the top ½ (¾, 1, 1½, 2, 2½)" of the side seam. Leave a gap of 1 (1, 1, 1 ½, 1½, 2, 2)", then sew the rest of the seam.

Switha Cushion

This simple stitch pattern is often used used in fishermen's ganseys. The pattern is pleasing on both sides of the fabric. Either can be used as the right side.

MATERIALS
100 (150, 200, 300) g aran weight yarn
pair 6 mm (US 10) needles
5 mm crochet hook for finishing
12 (14, 16,18)" square cushion pad
3 (4, 5, 5) buttons ½" diameter

SIZE
To fit: 12 (14, 16, 18)" cushion pad

TENSION
15 sts and 24 rows to 4" over pattern
after washing and blocking

FRONT
Cast on 42 (50, 58, 66) sts. Work in
pattern as follows:
Row 1: K.
Row 2: P.
Row 3: K2, [p2, k2] to the end.
Row 4: P2, [k2, p2] to the end.
Continue in pattern until the piece measures 11 (13, 15, 17)". Cast off.

BACK
Button piece:
Cast on 42 (50, 58, 66) sts and knit 7 (7,
9, 9) rows.
Work in pattern as for the front for 6 (8, 9,
10)". Cast off.

Buttonhole piece:
Cast on 42 (50, 58, 66) sts and knit 3 (3,
5, 5) rows.
Next Row: K2 (0, 3, 1), [k8 (8, 7, 9),
k2tog, yo] to last 10 sts, k10.
Knit 2 rows.

Work in pattern as for the front for 5 (5, 6, 7)".
Cast off.

FINISHING
Overlap the buttonhole section of the second back piece with the garter stitch border of the first piece. Tack together. Join the front and back pieces together either by slip stitch or using double crochet. Wash and dry flat. Remove tacking, and sew on buttons.

Flotta Cushion

This pattern also uses stitch patterns from fishermen's sweaters, or ganseys. A crisp yarn makes the pattern stand out.

MATERIALS
100 (150, 200, 300) g aran weight yarn
pair 6 mm (US 10) needles
5 mm crochet hook for finishing
12 (14, 16,18)" square cushion pad

SIZE
To fit: 12 (14, 16, 18)" cushion pad

TENSION
15 sts and 24 rows to 4" over pattern after washing and blocking

PATTERN

FRONT
Cast on 40 (50, 58, 66) sts.
Work from the chart for your size of cushion pad for 11 (13, 15, 17)". Cast off in pattern.

BACK
Make a second piece the same for the back.

FINISHING
Using whip stitch
With wrong sides together, carefully sew three sides of the cover together, insert the cushion pad, and sew up the fourth side. Weave in all ends.

Using crochet
With wrong sides together, work a row of double crochet, picking up loops from both front and back of cushion. Complete three sides, insert the cushion pad, and work the fourth side. Weave in all ends.

CHARTS

CHART FOR 12" CUSHION

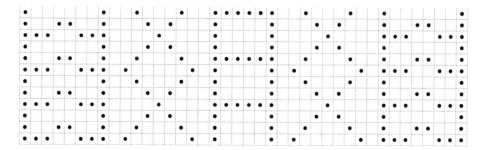

CHART FOR 14" CUSHION

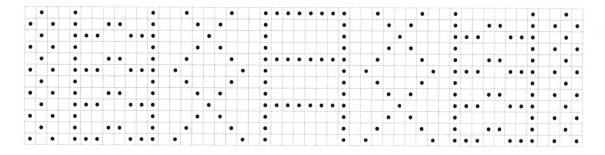

CHART FOR 16" CUSHION

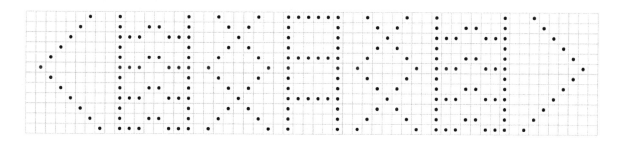

CHART FOR 18" CUSHION

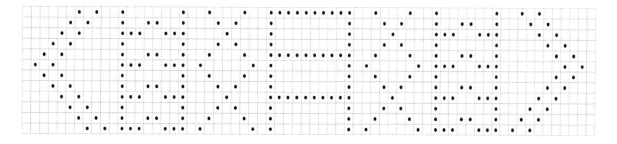

Cat's Paw Wrap

A simple but effective wrap using Cat's Paw and Old Shale Stitches. The centre panel of the wrap is knitted first followed by one end. Stitches are then picked up along the cast on edge to work the other end panel.

MATERIALS

300 gm North Ronaldsay fine yarn
pair 6 mm (US 10) needles
waste yarn for provisional cast on

SIZE

28" wide and 66" long
Length easily adjustable.

TENSION

16 sts and 20 rows to 4" over centre
pattern after washing and blocking

PATTERN

CENTRE

With waste yarn, cast on 111 sts.
Change to main yarn.
Work through the 6 rows of the Cat's
Paw Chart 34 times. *Adjust Centre
length here.*

FIRST END PANEL

Next row: K10, m1, k45, m1, k46, m1,
k10. 114 sts
Next row: K3, *yo, p2tog. Repeat from
* to last 3 sts, k3.
Work through the 4 rows of the Old
Shale Chart 15 times. *Adjust length
here.*
Knit 4 rows. Cast off very loosely.

SECOND END PANEL

Return to the provisional cast on and
place the stitches on the needle,
removing the waste yarn. 111 sts
Complete as for the First End Panel.

FINISHING

Weave in ends. Wash and block.

CHARTS

CAT'S PAW CHART

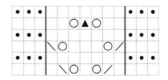

Row 1: K3, *k1, k2tog, yo, k1, yo,
k2togtbl, k1. Repeat from * to last 3 sts,
k3.
Row 2: K3, p to last 3 sts, k3.
Row 3: K3, *k2tog, yo, k3, yo, k2togtbl.
Repeat from * to last 3 sts, k3.
Row 4: As Row 2.
Row 5: K3, *k2, yo, k3tog, yo, k2. Re-
peat from * to last 3 sts, k3.
Row 6: As Row 2.

OLD SHALE CHART

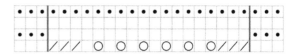

Row 1: K3, *k2tog 3 times, [yo, k1] 6
times, k2tog 3 times. Repeat from * to
last 3 sts, k3.
Row 2: K3, p to last 3 sts, k3.
Row 3: K.
Row 4: K.

Simple Lacy Sweaters

If you have knitted a snood or scarf, one of these jumpers or tunics could be your next project. There is no shaping in the lacy bits and the front and back are the same. The jumpers are shaped with rib at the bottom, while the tunics are straight up and down. Both styles have a boat neck. Still stylish after 20 years!

MATERIALS

300 (300, 350, 350, 400, 400, 450, 500, 550, 600) g North Ronaldsay fine yarn.
pairs 3.75 and 6 mm (US 5 and 10) needles

ACTUAL SIZES

To Fit Bust: 30 (32, 34, 38, 40, 44, 46, 50, 53, 56)"
Actual Bust: 32½ (36, 39, 42, 45, 48½, 52, 55, 58, 61½)"
Length Tunic: 25 (25, 26, 26, 27, 27, 28, 28, 29, 29)"
Length Jumper: 23 (23, 24, 24, 25, 25, 26, 26, 27, 27)"
Sleeve length: 15 (15, 16, 16, 17, 17, 18, 18, 19, 19)"
Length and sleeve length adjustable.

TENSION

15 sts and 24 rows to 4" over pattern on larger needles after washing and blocking

THE TUNIC

BACK AND FRONT

With smaller needles cast on 61 (67, 73, 79, 85, 91, 97, 103, 109, 115) sts. Knit 9 rows.
Change to larger needles. Work from the Razor Shell or Miniature Leaf Chart until the piece measures 24 (24, 25, 25, 26, 26, 27, 27, 28, 28)". *Adjust length here.*
Change to smaller needles. Knit 10 rows. Cast off using a larger needle.

Make a second piece the same.

SLEEVES

With smaller needles cast on 37 (37, 41, 41, 45, 45, 49, 49, 53, 53) sts. Knit 9 rows.

Next row: K1, (m1, k2) to end of row. 55 (55, 61, 61, 67, 67, 73, 73, 79, 79) sts
Change to larger needles and purl one row.
Work from the same chart as for the Front and Back until the piece measures 15 (15, 16, 16, 17, 17, 18, 18, 19, 19)". *Adjust length here.*
Cast off loosely.

THE JUMPER

BACK AND FRONT

With smaller needles cast on 61 (67, 73, 79, 85, 91, 97, 103, 109, 115) sts.
Row 1: K1, [p1, k1] to end of row.
Row 2: P1, [k1, p1] to end of row.
Repeat Rows 1 and 2 6 (6, 7, 7, 8, 8, 9, 9, 10, 10) times more.
Change to larger needles. Work from the Razor Shell or Miniature Leaf Chart until the piece measures 22 (22, 23, 23, 24, 24, 25, 25, 26, 26)". *Adjust length here.*
Change to smaller needles. Knit 10 rows. Cast off using a larger needle.

Make a second piece the same.

SLEEVES

With smaller needles cast on 37 (37, 41, 41, 45, 45, 49, 49, 53, 53) sts
Row 1: K1, [p1, k1] to end of row.
Row 2: P1, [k1, p1] to end of row.
Repeat Rows 1 and 2 6 (6, 7, 7, 8, 8, 9, 9, 10, 10) times more.
Next row: K1, (m1, k2) to end of row. 55 (55, 61, 61, 67, 67, 73, 73, 79, 79) sts
Complete as for the sleeves of the Tunic.

FINISHING

With the right sides of the Back and the Front together, pin shoulders together at the side edges. Place another pin 4 (4½, 5, 5½, 6, 6½, 7, 7½, 8, 8½)" from the edge. Repeat for the other shoulder.

Sew shoulders, leaving the neck open. Fold the sleeve in half lengthways and mark the centre of the cast off edge. With right sides together, pin this point to the shoulder seam. Pin the rest of top of sleeve to the sides of the front and back. Sew in carefully, but not too tightly. Sew in other sleeve. Sew side and sleeve seams.

Weave in all ends. Wash and block to size.

CHARTS

RAZOR SHELL CHART

Row 1: *K1, yo, k1, k3togtbl, k1, yo. Repeat from * to last st, k1.
Row 2: P.

MINIATURE LEAF CHART

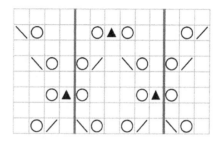

Row 1: K1, yo, ssk, *k1, k2tog, yo, k1, yo, ssk. Repeat from * to last 4sts, k1, k2tog, yo, k1.
Row 2 and all alternate rows: P.
Row 3: K2, yo, *k3tog, yo, k3. yo. Repeat from * to last 5 sts, k3tog, yo, k2.
Row 5: K1, k2tog, yo, *k1, yo, ssk, k1, k2tog, yo. Repeat from * to last 4 sts, k1, yo, ssk, k1.
Row 7: K2tog, yo, k1, *k2, yo, k3tog, yo, k1. Repeat from * to last 4 sts, k2, yo, ssk.
Row 8: P.

Lacy Scarves

If you have never tried lacy knitting, these patterns are for you. Scarves are a great way of trying out a stitch pattern new to you as the exact size doesn't matter. The scarves are worked on a garter stitch ground (to be reversible).

MATERIALS
60 (70, 80) g North Ronaldsay fine yarn
pair 6 mm (US 10) needles

SIZES
Width: 6 (8,10)" wide and
Length: 40 (50, 60)"
Length easily adjustable.

TENSION
New Shell: 18 sts and 34 rows to 4"
over pattern after washing and blocking
Horseshoe: 18 sts and 22 rows to 4"
over pattern after washing and blocking
Miniature Leaf: 18 sts and 20 rows to
4" over pattern after washing and
blocking
Note that tension is not crucial.

NEW SHELL SCARF
Cast on 27 (37, 47) sts loosely. Knit 5
rows.
Work from the New Shell Scarf Chart for
39 (49, 59)" or the desired length, ending after Row 1.
Knit 5 rows. Cast off loosely.

HORSESHOE SCARF
Cast on 27 (37, 47) sts loosely. Knit 5
rows.
Work from the Horseshoe Scarf Chart
for 39 (49, 59)" or the desired length,
ending after Row 7.
Knit 5 rows. Cast off loosely.

MINIATURE LEAF SCARF
Cast on 31 (37, 43) sts loosely. Knit 5
rows.

Work from the Miniature Leaf Scarf
Chart for 39 (49, 59)" or the desired
length, ending after Row 7.
Knit 5 rows. Cast off loosely.

FINISHING
Weave in ends. Wash and block.

CHARTS

NEW SHELL SCARF CHART

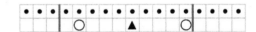

Row 1: K4, *yo, k3, k3togtbl, k3, yo, k1.
Repeat from * to last 3 sts, k3.
Row 2: K.

HORSESHOE SCARF CHART

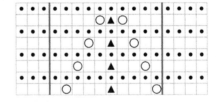

Row 1: K4, *yo, k3, k3togtbl, k3, yo, k1.
Repeat from * to last 3 sts, k3.
Row 2 and all even numbered rows:
K.
Row 3: K4, *k1, yo, k2, k3togtbl, k2, yo,
k2. Repeat from * to last 3 sts, k3.
Row 4: K4, *k2, yo, k1, k3togtbl, k1, yo,
k3. Repeat from * to last 3 sts, k3.
Row 7: K4, *k3, yo, k3togtbl, yo, k4.
Repeat from * to last 3 sts, k3.
Row 8: K.

MINIATURE LEAF SCARF CHART

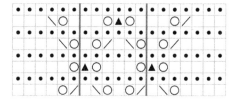

Row 2 and all even-numbered Rows: K.

Row 3: K5, yo, k3togtbl, *yo, k3, yo, k3togtbl. Repeat from * to last 5 sts, yo, k5.

Row 5: K4, k2tog, yo, k1, *yo, ssk, k1, k2tog, yo, k1. Repeat from * to last 6 sts, yo, ssk, k4.

Row 7: K3, k2tog, yo, k2, *k1, yo, k3togtbl, yo, k2. Repeat from * to last 6 sts, k1, yo, ssk, k3.

Row 8: K.

Row 1: K4, yo, ssk, k1, *k2tog, yo, k1, yo, ssk, k1. Repeat from * to last 6 sts, k2tog, yo, k4.

29

Lacy Cowls

MATERIALS

80 g North Ronaldsay fine yarn for the Miniature Leaf and Horseshoe Cowls
130 g North Ronaldsay fine yarn for the New Shell Cowl
6 mm (US 10) circular needle

SIZES

Circumference: 30" or 60"
Depth: 14" or 7"
Depth is easily adjustable.

TENSION

Miniature Leaf: 16 sts and 20 rows to 4" over pattern after washing and blocking.

Horseshoe: 16 sts and 22 rows to 4" over pattern after washing and blocking.

New Shell: 16 sts and 34 rows to 4" over pattern after washing and blocking.

PATTERN

Cast on 120 (240) sts loosely and join into a circle. Starting with a purl round, work 3 rounds in garter stitch.

Work in desired stitch pattern for about 14 (7)", finishing at the end of the chart. *Adjust depth here.* Staring with a purl round, work 3 rounds in garter stitch. Cast off loosely.

FINISHING
Weave in ends. Wash and block.

CHARTS

NEW SHELL COWL CHART

Rnd 1: *Yo, k3, k3togtbl, k3, yo, k1. Repeat from * to end of rnd.
Rnd 2: K.

HORSESHOE COWL CHART

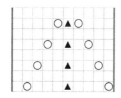

Rnd 1: *Yo, k3, k3togtbl, k3, yo, k1. Repeat from * to end of rnd.
Rnd 2 and all even-numbered Rnds: K.
Rnd 3: *K1, yo, k2, k3togtbl, k2, yo, k2. Repeat from * to end of rnd.
Rnd 5: *K2, yo, k1, k3togtbl, k1, yo, k3. Repeat from * to end of rnd.
Rnd 7: *K3, yo, k3togtbl, yo, k4. Repeat from * to end of rnd.
Rnd 8: K.

MINIATURE LEAF COWL CHART

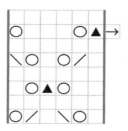

Rnd 1: *K1, yo, ssk, k1, k2tog, yo. Repeat from * to end of rnd.
Rnd 2 and all even-numbered Rnds: K.
Rnd 3: *K2, yo, k3togtbl, yo, k1. Repeat from * to end of rnd.
Rnd 5: *K1, k2tog, yo, k1, yo, ssk. Repeat from * to end of rnd.
Rnd 7: Mmr, *k3togtbl, yo, k3, yo. Repeat from * to end of rnd.
Rnd 8: K.

Cowls make a stylish and warm addition to your wardrobe, and make great presents. These are worked in the round on a stocking stitch ground and instructions are given for a short and a long loop.

Lacy Cushion Covers

The cover will be slightly smaller than the pad on the needles,
but will stretch to fit.

MATERIALS

For each cushion:
80 (100) g North Ronaldsay fine yarn
pair 6 mm needles
crochet hook size 10 mm for finishing if
required
16 (18)" square cushion pad

ACTUAL SIZE

To fit: 16 (18)" cushion pad

SHETLAND EYELET CUSHION

Cast on 58 (65) sts VERY LOOSELY and
knit 1 row.
Work from the Shetland Eyelet Chart for
a total of 92 (100) rows.
Cast off very loosely.
Make a second piece the same.

FIR CONE CUSHION

Cast on 61 (71) sts VERY LOOSELY and
knit 1 row.
Work from the Fir Cone Chart for your
size for a total of 100 (120) rows.
Cast off very loosely.
Make a second piece the same.

CAT'S PAW STRIPE CUSHION

Cast on 65 sts (for both sizes) VERY
LOOSELY and knit 1 row.
Work from the Cat's Paw Stripe Chart for
a total of 88 (96) rows.
Cast off very loosely.
Make a second piece the same.

TENSION

Shetland Eyelet Cushion: 15 sts and
24 rows to 4" after washing and blocking

Fir Cone Cushion: 17 sts and 28 rows
to 4" after washing and blocking

Cat's paw Stripe Cushion: 15 sts and
24 rows to 4" after washing and blocking

ALL CUSHIONS

FINISHING

Wash the pieces AND ENOUGH YARN
FOR SEWING UP. Pin to size and allow
to dry.

Using slip stitch:
With WRONG sides together, carefully
sew three sides of the cover together.
Insert the cushion pad; sew up the fourth
side.

Using crochet:
With wrong sides together, work a row
of double crochet, picking up loops from
both front and back of cushion. Work
very loosely, with the work under tension.
(If you find this difficult, use a very large
crochet hook!)   Complete three sides,
insert the cushion pad, and work the
fourth side.

SHETLAND EYELET CUSHION CHART

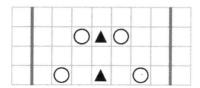

Row 1: K1, *k1, yo, k1, k3togtbl, k1, yo, k1. Repeat from * to last st, k1.
Row 2: P.
Row 3: K1, *k2, yo, k3togtbl, yo, k2. Repeat from * to last st, k1.
Row 4: P.

FIR CONE CUSHION CHART

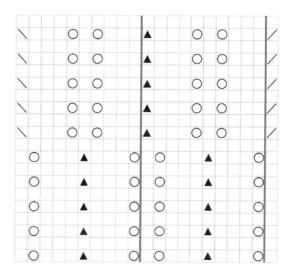

Row 1: K1, *yo, k3, k3togtbl, k3, yo, k1. Repeat from * to end of row.
Row 2: P.
Rows 3 to 10: Repeat Rows 1 and 2 four times more.
Row 11: K2tog, *k3, yo, k1, yo, k3, k3togtbl. Repeat from * to last 9 sts, k3, yo, k1, yo, k3, ssk.
Row 12: P.
Rows 13 to 20: Repeat Rows 11 and 12 four times more.

CAT'S PAW STRIPE CUSHION CHART

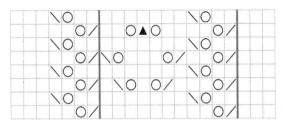

Row 1: K3, *k2tog, yo, k9. Repeat from * to last 7 sts, k2tog, yo, k5.

Row 2 and all alternate rows: P3, p2tog, yo, p2, *p7, p2tog, yo, p2. Repeat from * to last 3 sts, p3.

Row 3: K3, *k2tog, yo, k3, k2tog, yo, k1, yo, ssk, k1. Repeat from * to last 7 sts, k2tog, yo, k5.

Row 5: K3, *k2tog, yo, k2, k2tog, yo, k3, yo, ssk. Repeat from * to last 7 sts, k2tog, yo, k5.

Row 7: K3, *k2tog, yo, k4, yo, k3togtbl, yo, k2. Repeat from * to last 7 sts, k2tog, yo, k5.

Row 8: As Row 2

Cat's Paw Stripe Scarf

MATERIALS
80 g skein of North Ronaldsay fine yarn
Two 6 mm (US 10) needles
tapestry needle

SIZE
8" wide and 56" long
Length is easily adjustable.

TENSION
15 sts and 24 rows to 4" after washing
and blocking

PATTERN

With 6 mm needles, cast on 32 sts
loosely. Knit 5 rows.

Work from the Cat's Paw Stripe Cushion
Chart (opposite) for desired length, ending after a Row 1.

Knit 5 rows. Cast off loosely.

FINISHING
Weave in ends. Wash and block.

Sampler Throw

These are old Shetland patterns. They were used to make garments to sell, and therefore it was important that the patterns, while looking complex, were actually straightforward to knit. The women and girls would knit anywhere and everywhere, so they could not rely on written instructions: the next row had to follow on instinctively.

New Shell and Razor Shell are two row patterns, one of which is purl. Cat's paw is a six row pattern, three of which are purl. Horseshoe and miniature leaf are eight row patterns, including four purl rows. Fir cone is a twenty row pattern, but with only two pattern rows to remember. All the patterns can be made "double sided" by knitting the alternate rows rather than purling.

The squares can be different colours or the same, and the patterns can be different or the same. Once all the squares have been made, crochet or sew them together and add the border.

Each 12" square takes about 35 g wool, and the border about 80 g. If using more than one pattern or colour, it is an idea to plan your throw before you start. The border works well in a single colour or stripes using left over yarn. If using different colours, work one or two pattern repeats in each colour.

MATERIALS

400 g North Ronaldsay fine yarn
pair 6 mm (US 10) needles
100 cm or longer circular 6 mm (US 10) needle
crochet hook size about 5 for finishing if required

ACTUAL SIZE

About 48" square for a nine-square blanket

TENSION

16 sts to 4" over most patterns after washing and blocking. The row tension varies and is not critical.

INDIVIDUAL SQUARES

Make 9 squares. There are 7 stitch patterns. Repeat the ones you like best!

NEW SHELL, HORSESHOE AND FIRCONE

Cast on 47 sts loosely and knit 5 rows. Work though the appropriate chart until the work measures 11½" when stretched to 12" wide, preferably finishing with the last row of the chart. Knit 5 rows. Cast off very loosely.

RAZOR SHELL AND MINIATURE LEAF

Cast on 49 sts loosely and knit 5 rows. Work though the appropriate chart until the work measures 11½" when slightly stretched, preferably finishing with the last row of the chart. Knit 5 rows. Cast off very loosely.

CAT'S PAW

Cast on 48 sts loosely and knit 5 rows. Work though the Cat's Paw Chart until the work measures 11½" when slightly stretched, preferably finishing with the last row of the chart. Knit 5 rows. Cast off very loosely.

SHETLAND EYELET

Cast on 50 sts loosely and knit 5 rows. Work though the Shetland Eyelet chart until the work measures 11½" when slightly stretched, preferably finishing with the last row of the chart. Knit 5 rows. Cast off very loosely.

BORDER

Sew or crochet the squares together.

With the circular needle, and starting from one corner with RSF, pick up and knit stitches round the edge as follows: *pick up and knit 144 sts evenly along one edge (48 per square), PM, pick up 1 st from the corner, PM. Repeat from * three times more.
Round 1: *Work the first round of the Old Shale Chart eight times, SM, work the first round of the Old Shale Corner Chart. Repeat from * three times more.
Round 2: *Work the second round of the Old Shale Chart eight times, SM, work the second round of the Old Shale Corner Chart. Repeat from * three times more.

Continue in this way until the corner chart has been finished, repeating the 4 rows of the Old Shale Chart as required.

Cast off very loosely.

FINISHING

Weave in all ends. Wash and block, pinning out each scallop of the border.

CHARTS

NEW SHELL CHART

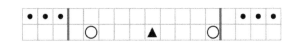

Row 1: K4, *yo, k3, k3togtbl, k3, yo, k1. Repeat from * to last 3 sts, k3.
Row 2: K3, p to last 3 sts, k3.

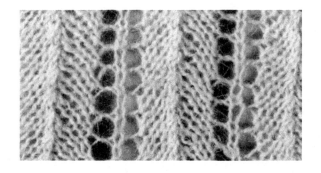

HORSESHOE CHART

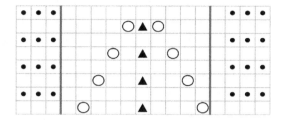

Row 1: K4, *yo, k3, k3togtbl, k3, yo, k1.
Repeat from * to last 3 sts, k3.
Row 2 and all even numbered rows:
K3, p to last 3 sts, k3.
Row 3: K4, *k1, yo, k2, k3togtbl, k2, yo,
k2. Repeat from * to last 3 sts, k3.
Row 5: K4, *k2, yo, k1, k3togtbl, k1, yo,
k3. Repeat from * to last 3 sts, k3.
Row 7: K4, *k3, yo, k3togtbl, yo, k4.
Repeat from * to last 3 sts, k3.
Row 8: As Row 2.

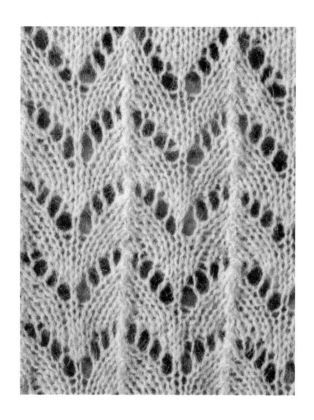

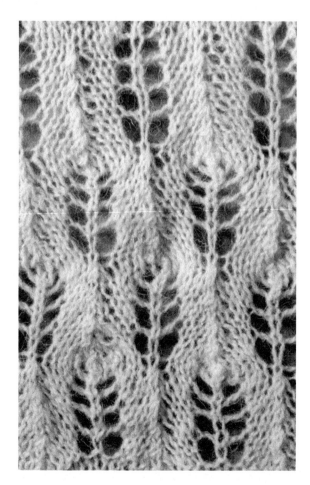

FIRCONE CHART

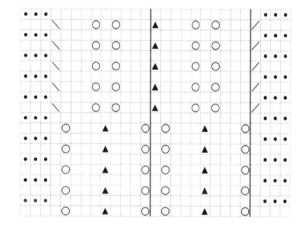

Row 1: K4, *yo, k3, k3togtbl, k3, yo, k1.
Repeat from * to last 3 sts, k3.
Row 2: K3, p to last 3 sts, k3.
Rows 3 to 10: Repeat Rows 1 and 2
four times more.
Row 11: K3, k2tog, *k3, yo, k1, yo, k3,
k3togtbl. Repeat from * to last 12 sts,
k3, yo, k1, yo, k3, ssk, k3.
Row 12: As Row 2.
Rows 13 to 20: Repeat Rows 11 and
12 four times more.

RAZOR SHELL CHART

Row 1: K4, *yo, k1, k3togtbl, k1, yo, k1.
Repeat from * to last 3 sts, k3.
Row 2: K3, p to last 3 sts, k3.

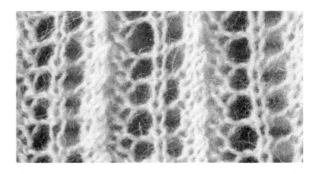

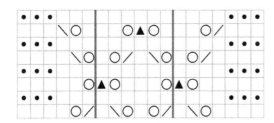

SHETLAND EYELET CHART

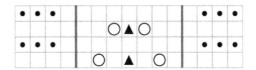

Row 1: K4, *k1, yo, k1, k3togtbl, k1, yo, k1. Repeat from * to last 4 sts, k4.
Row 2: K4, p to last 3 sts, k3.
Row 3: K3, *k2, yo, k3togtbl, yo, k2. Repeat from * to last 4 sts, k4.
Row 4: As Row 2.

MINIATURE LEAF CHART

Row 1: K4, yo, ssk, k1, *k2tog, yo, k1, yo, ssk, k1. Repeat from * to last 6 sts, k2tog, yo, k4.
Row 2 and all even numbered rows: K3, p to last 3 sts, k3.
Row 3: K5, yo, k3togtbl, *yo, k3, yo, k3togtbl. Repeat from * to last 5 sts, yo, k5.
Row 5: K4, k2tog, yo, k1, *yo, ssk, k1, k2tog, yo, k1. Repeat from * to last 6 sts, yo, ssk, k4.
Row 7: K3, k2tog, yo, k2, *k1, yo, k3togtbl, yo, k2. Repeat from * to last 6 sts, k1, yo, ssk, k3.
Row 8: As Row 2.

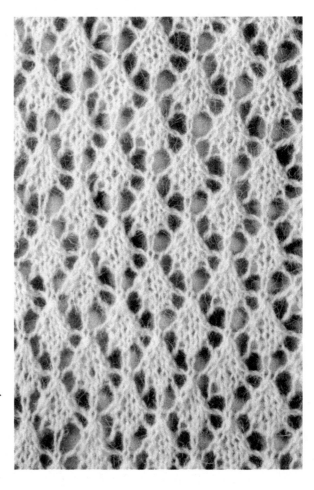

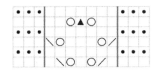

Row 1: K3, *k1, k2tog, yo, k1, yo, ssk, k1. Repeat from * to last 3 sts, k3.
Row 2 and all even numbered rows: K3, p to last 3 sts, k3.
Row 3: K3, *k2tog, yo, k3, yo, ssk. Repeat from * to last 3 sts, k3.
Row 5: K3, *k2, yo, k3togtbl, yo, k2. Repeat from * to last 3 sts, k3.
Row 6: As Row 2.

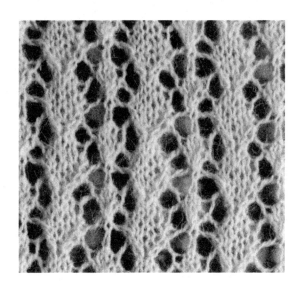

OLD SHALE CHART

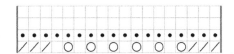

Rnd 1: K2tog three times, [yo, k1] six times, k2tog three times.
Rnd 2: P.
Rnds 3 and 4: K.

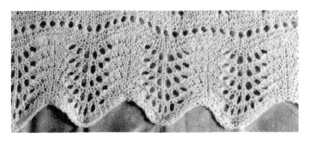

OLD SHALE CORNER CHART

Rnd 1: Yo, k1, yo.
Rnd 2: P.
Rnd 3: (K1, yo) twice, k1.
Rnd 4: K.
Rnd 5: K2, yo, k1, yo, k2.
Rnd 6: P.
Rnd 7: K3, yo, k1, yo, k3.
Rnd 8: K.
Rnd 9: K4, yo, k1, yo, k4.
Rnd 10: P.
Rnd 11: K5, yo, k1, yo, k5.
Rnd 12: K.
Rnd 13: K2tog, (k1, yo, k3, yo) twice, k1, k2tog.
Rnd 14: P.
Rnd 15: K7, yo, k1, yo, k7.
Rnd 16: K.
Rnd 17: K2tog twice, (yo, k1, yo, k3) twice, yo, k1, yo, k2tog twice.
Rnd 18: P.
Rnd 19: K9, yo, k1, yo, k9.

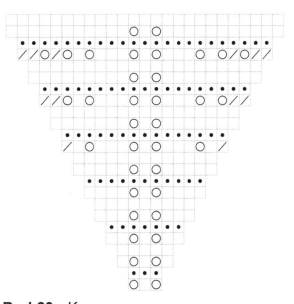

Rnd 20: K.
Rnd 21: K2tog twice, yo, k2tog, (yo, k1, yo, k3) twice, yo, k1, yo, k2tog, yo, k2tog twice.
Rnd 22: P.
Rnd 23: K11, yo, k1, yo, k11.
Rnd 24: K.

Stocking Stitch Top

This simple top with small side slits pops effortlessly over tee shirts or roll necks.
If you want a looser fit, knit the next size up.

MATERIALS
170 (200, 240, 280, 320, 370, 440, 500,
570) g North Ronaldsay fine yarn
pairs 4 and 5 mm (US 6 and 8) needles
row counter
stitch holders or lengths of spare yarn

ACTUAL SIZES
To fit bust: 28 (32, 36, 40, 44, 48, 52,
56, 60)"
Actual size: 31 (35½, 40, 44½, 49, 53½,
58, 62, 65½)"
Length: 19 (20, 21, 21, 22, 22, 23, 23,
24)"
Sleeve: 15 (15, 16, 17, 18, 18, 19, 20,
20)"
Length and sleeve length adjustable.

TENSION
18 sts and 24 rows to 4" with larger
needles over stocking stitch after
washing and blocking

PATTERN

BACK
With 5 mm needles, cast on 70 (80, 90,
100, 110, 120, 130, 140, 150) sts loosely.
Rows 1 to 3: S1p, k to end of row.
Work slit border as follows:
Row 4: S1p, k to end of row.
Row 5: S1p, k2, p to last 3 sts, k3.
Rows 6 to 15: Repeat Rows 4 and 5 five
times more.
Continue in stocking stitch until the work
measures 13". *Adjust length here.*

Shape armhole:
Rows 1 and 2: Cast off 2 (3, 4, 6, 10,
13, 17, 21, 25), k to end of row.

Row 3: K2togtbl, k to last 2 sts, k2tog.
Row 4: P2tog, p to last 2 sts, p2togtbl.
Rows 5 and 6: Repeat Rows 3 and 4.
Row 7: As Row 3.
Row 8: P.
Repeat Rows 7 and 8 1 (2, 2, 3, 3, 4, 4,
4, 4) times more. 54 (62, 68, 72, 74, 76,
78, 80, 82) sts

Work straight until the piece measures 5
(5½, 6, 6, 6½, 6½, 7, 7, 8)" from the start
of the armhole shaping.

Shape neck:
Row 1: K20 (21, 25, 27, 29, 29, 30, 30, 31), k2tog. Turn. Work on these sts only.
Row 2: P2tog, p to end of row.
Row 3: K to last 2 sts, k2tog.
Rows 4 and 5: As Rows 2 and 3.
Row 6: As Row 2. 16 (17, 21, 23, 25, 25, 26, 26, 27) sts
Work a further 0 (2, 6, 6, 8, 10, 12, 12, 12) rows straight.
Cast off

Return to held sts.
Place the next 14 (16, 18, 20, 22, 24, 24, 26, 26) sts on a yarn holder. 22 (23, 27, 29, 31, 31, 32, 32, 33) sts remain.
Work these sts as follows:
Row 1: K2tog, k to the end of row.
Row 2: P to last 2 sts, p2togtbl.
Rows 3 to 6: Repeat Rows 1 and 2 twice more. 16 (17, 21, 23, 25, 25, 26, 26, 27) sts
Work a further 0 (2, 6, 6, 8, 10, 12, 12, 12) rows straight.
Cast off.

FRONT

Work as for the back until the armhole shaping has been completed finishing after a purl row. 54 (62, 68, 72, 74, 76, 78, 80, 82) sts
Next Row: K.
Next Row: P23 (27, 30, 32, 33, 34, 35, 36, 37), k8, p to end of row.
Repeat these 2 rows once more.

Split for the neck:
Row 1: K27 (31, 34, 36, 37, 38, 39, 40, 41). Turn. Place the remaining sts on a yarn holder
Row 2: S1p, k3, p to the end of the row.
Row 3: K.
Repeat Rows 2 and 3 until the piece measures 4" from the start of the arm-hole shaping, finishing after a purl row.

NECK

Sew up both shoulder seams.
With right side facing and smaller needles, place the 6 (9, 8, 8, 7, 8, 8, 9, 9) sts from the holder on the left front on to one needle. Rejoin yarn. Pick up and knit 9 (12, 15, 16, 18, 19, 21, 24, 27) sts from the left front neck and 7 (8, 11, 12, 13, 14, 15, 15, 15) from the left back neck; knit 14 (16, 18, 20, 22, 24, 24, 26, 26) from the back neck; pick up and knit 7 (8, 11, 12, 13, 14, 15, 15, 15) from the right back neck and 9 (12, 15, 16, 18, 19, 21, 24, 27) from the right front; then knit 6 (9, 8, 8, 7, 8, 8, 9, 9) from the right front. 58 (74, 86, 92, 98, 106, 112, 122, 128) sts
Row 1: S1p, k1, k2tog, yo, k to end of row.
Rows 2 to 5: S1p, k to end of row.
Cast off using a larger needle.

SLEEVES

With 5 mm needles, cast on 30 (32, 34, 36, 40, 44, 50, 58, 66) sts. Knit 3 rows.
Work 16 (16, 16, 16, 10, 6, 2, 2, 2) rows in stocking stitch.
Increase as follows:
Row 1: K1, m1, k to last st, m1, k1.
Rows 2 to 4: In stocking stitch.
Repeat Rows 1 to 4 until there are 54 (60, 66, 72, 82, 90, 100, 110, 120) sts on the needle.
Work straight until the sleeve seam measures 15 (15, 16, 17, 18, 18, 19, 20, 20)". *Adjust length here.*

Shape top:
Row 1: Cast off 2 (3, 4, 6, 10, 13, 17, 21, 25), k to end of row.
Row 2: Cast off 2 (3, 4, 6, 10, 13, 17, 21, 25), p to end of row. 50 (54, 58, 60, 62, 64, 66, 68, 70) sts
Row 3: K2togtbl, k to last 2 sts, k2tog.
Row 4: P2tog, p to last 2 sts, p2togtbl.
Rows 5 and 6: Repeat Rows 3 and 4.

Row 7: As Row 3.
Row 8: P.
Work 0 (1, 2, 4, 6, 8, 10, 12, 14) rows straight.
Repeat Rows 7 and 8 five times more.
Repeat Rows 3 and 4 twice.
Next Row: Cast off 4 sts, k to end of row.
Next Row: Cast off 4 sts, p to end of row. 14 (18, 22, 24, 26, 28, 30, 32, 34) sts

Repeat these two rows 0 (1, 1, 2, 2, 2, 3, 3, 3) times more.
Cast off remaining sts.

Work a second sleeve to match.

FINISHING
Sew up sleeve seams. Sew up side seams, starting from the end of the garter stitch border to the side slits. Set in the sleeves. Sew button on neck to correspond with the buttonhole.

End-to-End Crescent

Made from one skein of yarn, this stylish scarf can be worn in several ways.

MATERIALS

100 g North Ronaldsay fine yarn
pair 6 mm needles

SIZE

14" wide and 60" long

TENSION

16 sts and 22 rows to 4" after washing
and blocking

*Note that the stitch marker comes
between the lace edging and the main
shawl. Shaping is all in the main shawl.*

PATTERN

Cast on 4 sts.
Set Up Row: K2, PM, k2.

Work through the Initial Tip Chart,
noting that the marker comes between
the lace edging and the garter stitch
section.
Work through the Increase Chart four
times.
Work through the Central Section Chart
four times.
Work through the Decrease Chart four
times.
Work through the Final Tip Chart.
Cast off remaining 4 sts.

CHARTS

INITIAL TIP CHART

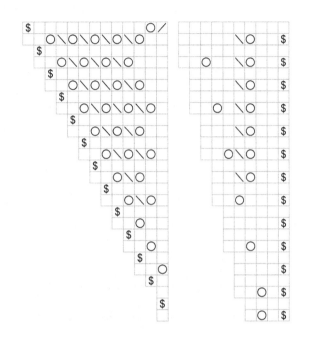

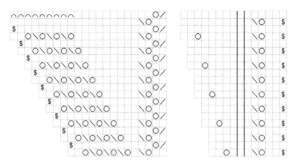

Row 1: S1p, k1, yo, k2.
Row 2 and all alternate rows: S1p, k to end of row.
Row 3: S1p, k1, yo, k3.
Row 5: S1p, k4, yo, k2.
Row 7: S1p, k2, yo, k3, yo, k2.
Row 9: S1p, k7, yo, k2.
Row 11: S1p, (k3, yo) twice, ssk, yo, k2.
Row 13: S1p, k2, yo, ssk, k4, yo, ssk, yo, k2.
Row 15: S1p, k2, yo, ssk, yo, k3, (yo, ssk) twice, yo, k2.
Row 17: S1p, k2, yo, ssk, k5, (yo, ssk) twice, yo, k2.
Row 19: S1p, k2, yo, ssk, k1, yo, k3, (yo, ssk) three times, yo, k2.
Row 21: S1p, k2, yo, ssk, k6, (yo, ssk) three times, yo, k2.
Row 23: S1p, k2, yo, ssk, k2, yo, k5, (yo, ssk) three times, yo, k2.
Row 25: S1p, k2, yo, ssk, k7, (yo, ssk) four times, yo, k2.
Row 26: S1p, k10, yo, ssk, PM, k10.

Row 1: S1p, k2, yo, ssk, k to 2 sts before M, yo, k4, yo, ssk, k1, (yo, ssk) three times, yo, k2.
Row 2: S1p, k11, yo, ssk, k to end of row.
Row 3: S1p, k2, yo, ssk, k to 2 sts after M, yo, ssk, k2, (yo, ssk) three times, yo, k2.
Row 4: S1p, k12, yo, ssk, k to end of row.
Row 5: S1p, k2, yo, ssk, k to 2 sts before M, yo, k4, yo, ssk, k3, (yo, ssk) three times, yo, k2.
Row 6: S1p, k13, yo, ssk, k to end of row.
Row 7: S1p, k2, yo, ssk, k to 2 sts after M, yo, ssk, k4, (yo, ssk) three times, yo, k2.
Row 8: S1p, k14, yo, ssk, k to end of row.
Row 9: S1p, k2, yo, ssk, k to 2 sts before M, yo, k4, yo, k4, yo, ssk, k5, (yo, ssk) three times, yo, k2.
Row 10: S1p, k15, yo, ssk, k to end of row.
Row 11: S1p, k2, yo, ssk, k to 2 sts after M, yo, ssk, k6, (yo, ssk) three times, yo, k2.
Row 12: S1p, k16, yo, ssk, k to end of row.
Row 13: S1p, k2, yo, ssk, k to 2 sts before M, yo, k4, yo, k4, yo, ssk, k7, (yo, ssk) three times, yo, k2.
Row 14: S1p, k17, yo, ssk, k to end of row.
Row 15: S1p, k2, yo, ssk, k to 2 sts after M, yo, ssk, k8, (yo, ssk) three times, yo, k2.

Row 16: S1p, k18, yo, ssk, k to end of row.
Row 17: S1p, k2, yo, ssk, k to 2 sts before M, yo, k4, yo, k4, yo, ssk, k9, (yo, ssk) three times, yo, k2.
Row 18: S1p, k19, yo, ssk, k to end of row.
Row 19: S1p, k2, yo, ssk, k to 2 sts after M, yo, ssk, k18.
Row 20: Cast off 9, k11, yo, ssk, k to end of row.

CENTRAL CHART

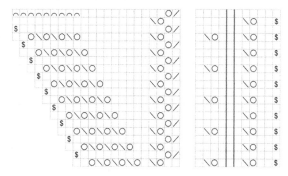

Row 1: S1p, k2, yo, ssk, k to 3 sts before M, yo, ssk, k3, yo, ssk, k1, (yo, ssk) three times, yo, k2.
Row 2: S1p, k11, yo, ssk, k to end of row.
Row 3: S1p, k2, yo, ssk, k, yo, ssk, k2, (yo, ssk) three times, yo, k2.
Row 4: S1p, k12, yo, ssk, k to end of row.
Row 5: S1p, k2, yo, ssk, k to 3 sts before M, yo, ssk, k3, yo, ssk, k3, (yo, ssk) three times, yo, k2. to 2 sts after M
Row 6: S1p, k13, yo, ssk, k to end of row.
Row 7: S1p, k2, yo, ssk, k to 2 sts after M, yo, ssk, k4, (yo, ssk) three times, yo, k2.
Row 8: S1p, k14, yo, ssk, k to end of row.
Row 9: S1p, k2, yo, ssk, k to 3 sts before M, yo, ssk, k3, yo, ssk, k5, (yo, ssk) three times, yo, k2.
Row 10: S1p, k15, yo, ssk, k to end of row.

Row 11: S1p, k2, yo, ssk, k to 2 sts after M, yo, ssk, k6, (yo, ssk) three times, yo, k2.
Row 12: S1p, k16, yo, ssk, k to end of row.
Row 13: S1p, k2, yo, ssk, k to 3 sts before M, yo, ssk, k3, yo, ssk, k7, (yo, ssk) three times, yo, k2.
Row 14: S1p, k17, yo, ssk, k to end of row.
Row 15: S1p, k2, yo, ssk, k to 2 sts after M, k8, (yo, ssk) three times, yo, k2.
Row 16: S1p, k18, yo, ssk, k to end of row.
Row 17: S1p, k2, yo, ssk, k to 3 sts before M, yo, ssk, k3, yo, ssk, k3, (yo, ssk) three times, yo, k2.
Row 18: S1p, k19, yo, ssk, k to end of row.
Row 19: S1p, k2, yo, ssk, k to 2 sts after M, yo, ssk, k18.
Row 20: Cast off 9, k11, yo, ssk, k to end of row.

DECREASE CHART

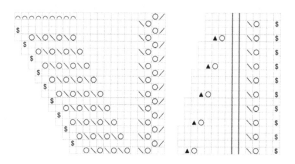

Row 1: S1p, k2, yo, ssk, k to 4 sts before M, yo, k3togtbl, k3, yo, ssk, k, (yo, ssk) three times, yo, k2.
Row 2: S1p, k11, yo, ssk, k15.
Row 3: S1p, k2, yo, ssk, k to 2 sts after M, yo, ssk, k2, (yo, ssk) three times, yo, k2.
Row 4: S1p, k12, yo, ssk, k15.
Row 5: S1p, k2, yo, ssk, k to 4 sts before M, yo, k3togtbl, (k3, yo, ssk) twice, (yo, ssk) twice, yo, k2.
Row 6: S1p, k13, yo, ssk, k14.

Row 7: S1p, k2, yo, ssk, k to 2 sts after M, yo, ssk, k4, (yo, ssk) three times, yo, k2.
Row 8: S1p, k14, yo, ssk, k14.
Row 9: S1p, k2, yo, ssk, k to 4 sts before M, yo, k3togtbl, k3, yo, ssk, k5, (yo, ssk) three times, yo, k2.
Row 10: S1p, k15, yo, ssk, k13.
Row 11: S1p, k2, yo, ssk, k to 2 sts after M, yo, ssk, k6, (yo, ssk) three times, yo, k2.
Row 12: S1p, k16, yo, ssk, k13.
Row 13: S1p, k2, yo, ssk, k to 4 sts before M, yo, k3togtbl, k3, yo, ssk, k7, (yo, ssk) three times, yo, k2.
Row 14: S1p, k17, yo, ssk, k12.
Row 15: S1p, k2, yo, ssk, k to 2 sts after M, yo, ssk, k8, (yo, ssk) three times, yo, k2.
Row 16: S1p, k18, yo, ssk, k12.
Row 17: S1p, k2, yo, ssk, k to 4 sts before M, yo, k3togtbl, k3, yo, ssk, k9, (yo, ssk) three times, yo, k2.
Row 18: S1p, k19, yo, ssk, k11.
Row 19: S1p, k2, yo, ssk, k to 2 sts after M, yo, ssk, k18.
Row 20: Cast off 9, k11, yo, ssk, k11.

FINAL TIP CHART

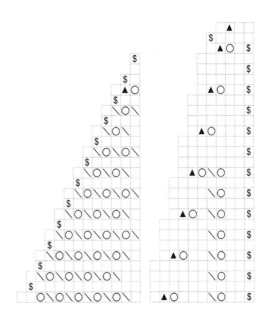

Row 1: S1p, k2, yo, ssk, k3, yo, k3togtbl, k2, (ssk, yo) five times, k2.
Row 2 and all alternate rows: S1p, k to end of row.
Row 3: S1p, k2, yo, ssk, k8, (ssk, yo) four times, ssk, k1.
Row 5: S1p, k2, yo, ssk, k2, yo, k3togtbl, k2, (ssk, yo) four times, ssk, k1.
Row 7: S1p, k2, yo, ssk, k5, (ssk, yo) four times, ssk, k1.
Row 9: S1p, k2, yo, ssk, k1, yo, k3togtbl, k2, (ssk, yo) three times, ssk, k1.
Row 11: S1p, k2, yo, ssk, k4, (ssk, yo) three times, ssk, k1.
Row 13: S1p, k2, yo, ssk, yo, k3togtbl, k2, (ssk, yo) twice, ssk, k1.
Row 15: S1p, k7, (ssk, yo) twice, ssk, k1.
Row 17: S1p, k3, yo, k3togtbl, k2, ssk, yo, ssk, k1.
Row 19: S1p, k6, ssk, yo, ssk, k1.
Row 21: S1p, k2, (yo, k3togtbl, k1) twice.
Row 23: S1p, k6.
Row 25: S1p, k, yo, k3togtbl, k1.
Row 27: K2, k3togtbl, k1.

Beret and Fingerless Mittens

Wear the hat as a beret or cloche – either way you will be both warm and stylish.

MATERIALS
For the hat:
30 (35, 40, 50, 65, 80) g fine North Ronaldsay yarn
2 cable needles about 3 mm for i-cord
6 stitch markers
For the mitts:
25 (30, 35, 40, 50, 65) g fine North Ronaldsay yarn
2 stitch markers
For either:
pair 3.25 mm (US 3) needles
row counter

SIZES

To fit: toddler (child, young teen, small adult, medium adult, large adult, extra large adult)
Head circumference: 17 (19, 21, 22, 23, 24)"
Palm circumference: 5 (5½, 6, 7, 8, 9)"

TENSION

26 sts and 36 rows to 4" over stocking stitch on larger needles after washing and blocking

BERET

Cast on 80 (94, 106, 116, 126, 134) sts.
Starting with a knit row, work in stocking stitch for 8 (8, 10, 10, 10, 10 ,10) rows then in k1, p1 rib for 6 (8, 10, 10, 10, 10) rows.
Increase row: K2 (2, 0, 0, 0, 0), *k1, m1, k1. Repeat from * to end of row. 119 (140, 159, 174, 189, 201) sts

Starting with a purl row, work 6 (8, 8,10, 12, 14) more rows in stocking stitch. (WSF for next row.)
Starting with a KNIT row, work 5 (5, 7, 7, 7, 7) rows in reverse stocking stitch.
Next Row (RSF): [P10, kfb] 0 (0, 2, 1, 0, 2) times, p to end of row. 119 (140, 161, 175, 189, 203) sts
Next Row: *PM, p17 (20, 23, 25, 27, 29). Repeat from * six times more.

Shape top:
Row 1: *K to 2 sts before M, k2tog, SM. Repeat five times more, k to last 2 sts, k2tog.
Row 2: P.
Repeat Rows 1 and 2 until 42 sts remain, finishing after a Row 1. (WSF for next row.)
Next Row: *P2tog, p4. Repeat from * to end of row.
Next Row: *K3, k2tog. Repeat from * to end of row.
Next Row: *P2tog, p2. Repeat from * to end of row.
Next Row: *K1, k2tog. Repeat from * to end of row, removing markers as you go.
Next Row: P2tog seven times.
Next Row: K2tog three times, k1.
Work i-cord (p 100) on the remaining 4 sts for 8 (8, 10, 10, 10, 10)".

FINISHING

Sew up back seam. Wash and dry flat.
Tie an overhand knot in the i-cord.

FINGERLESS MITTS

Cast on 30 (34, 36, 42, 48, 54) sts. Starting with a knit row, work in stocking stitch for 8 (8, 10, 10, 10 ,10) rows. Change to k1, p1 rib for 12 (14, 16, 18, 20, 22) rows. Change to stocking stitch and work 2 rows.

Thumb Gusset
Left Mitt:
Row 1: K17 (19, 20, 23, 26, 29), PM, m1, k2, m1, PM, k11 (13, 14, 17, 20, 23).
Right Mitt:
Row 1: K11 (13, 14, 17, 20, 23), PM, m1, k2, m1, PM, k17(19, 20, 23, 26, 29).

Both Mitts:
Rows 2 to 4: In stocking stitch.
Row 5: K to M, SM, m1, k4, m1, SM, k to end of row.
Rows 6 to 8: In stocking stitch.

Repeat rows 5 to 8 until 14 (18, 18, 22, 26, 30) rows have been worked and there are 10 (12, 12, 14, 16, 18) sts between the markers.
Next Row: K to second M, turn.
Next Row: P to M, turn.

Work 4 (6, 6, 6, 8, 8) rows more in stocking stitch on these 10 (12, 12, 14, 16, 18) sts. Cast off loosely. Sew up thumb seam.

With RSF, rejoin yarn to the base of the thumb. Pick up and knit 2 sts from the base of the thumb, then knit the rest of the row. 30 (34, 36, 42, 48, 54) sts Work 7 (7, 9, 9, 11, 11) rows in stocking stitch, then 2 (2, 4, 4, 6, 6) rows in k1, p1 rib, then 6 (6, 8, 8, 8, 8) rows in stocking stitch. Cast off.

FINISHING
Sew up side seam. Weave in all ends.

Roving Bags

If you do not spin, you can knit North Ronaldsay roving directly. Once knitted, your bag can be felted and/or lined with fabric.

MATERIALS

For the Kindle Bag:
pair 6 mm (US 10) needles
60 g roving
1 large button, about 25 mm (1") across
1 m (1 yd) chain for strap if required

For the Project Bag:
8mm (US 11) circular needle
120 g roving

SIZE

Kindle Bag: 6" by 10"
Project Bag: 8" by 12" excluding handles

TENSION

12 sts and 20 rows to 10 cm (4") over stocking stitch
Note that tension is not critical, but having a different tension will affect the size of the bags and the yardage needed.

First, prepare the roving for knitting as described on page 100.

KINDLE BAG

Cast on 7 sts and knit 3 rows.
Shape flap as follows:
Row 1: K 1, kfb, k to last 3 sts, kfb, k2.
Row 2: K2, p to last 2 sts, k2.
Row 3: K1, kfb, k1, k2tog, yo, k1, kfb, k2.
Row 4: As Row 2.
Repeat Rows 1 and 2 until there are 27 sts on the needle.

Work straight in stocking stitch for 10", finishing after a knit row.
Knit 1 row. Cast off.

PROJECT BAG

Cast on 31 sts.
Rows 1 to 3: K.
Row 4: K8, cast off 15, k8.
Row 5: K8, cast on 15, k8.
Rows 6 to 8: K.
Change to stocking stitch and increase as follows:
Row 1: K1, kfb, k to last 2 sts, kfb, k1.
Row 2: K2, p to last 2 sts, k2.
Repeat Rows 1 and 2 four times more. 41 sts
Break yarn and leave on a spare needle.

Make a second handle the same, but do not break yarn.

BODY
Rnd 1: K the sts from the second handle, then the sts from the first handle. Join to form a circle.
Rnd 2: K.
Repeat Round 2 until the bag measures 20 cm from the bottom of the garter stitch, or until your fibre runs out.
Cast off all stitches using a three needle cast off on the right side.

FINISHING
Weave in all ends.

V Necked Vest

470 (500, 530, 580, 640, 700) g aran weight yarn
pairs 4.5 and 5 mm needles (US 7 and 8)
4.5 mm (US 7) circular or dpns
thin needle for picking up stitches
1 stitch marker
row counter

SIZES

To fit chest: 32 (36, 40, 46, 50, 56)"
Actual size: 34 (40, 45, 51, 57, 62)"
Length: 24 (24½, 25, 26, 27, 28)"
Length easily adjustable.

TENSION

16 sts and 24 rows to 4" over pattern on larger needles after washing and blocking

BACK

With 4.5 mm needles, cast on 73 (85, 97, 109, 121, 133) sts.
Work in k1, p1 rib for 2.5 (2.5, 3, 3, 3, 3)".
Change to 5 mm needles and pattern.
Work from Chart 1 then Chart 2, repeating as necessary, until the piece measures 15" from the start, noting number of rows worked. *Adjust length here.*

Shape Armholes
Continue working from the chart and decrease as follows:
Row 1: K4 (6, 8, 10, 12, 14), put these sts on a thread; k2tog, work to last 6 (8, 10, 12, 14, 16) sts, k2togtbl, put remaining 4 (6, 8, 10, 12, 14) sts on a thread.
Row 2: P2togtbl, work to last 2 sts, p2tog.
Row 3: K2tog, work to last 2 sts, k2togtbl.
Repeat rows 2 and 3 three times more, then row 2 again. 45 (53, 61, 69, 77, 85) sts.

Now work straight until the work measures 9 (9½, 10, 11, 12, 13)" from the start of the armholes, noting the number of rows worked. Break yarn.
Place the sts on stitch holders as follows: 10 (11, 12, 14, 16, 18) for the first shoulder, 25 (31, 37, 41, 45, 49) for the back of the neck, 10 (11, 12, 14, 16, 18) for the second shoulder.

FRONT

Work as for the back to the armholes.

Shape Armholes
Row 1: K4 (6, 8, 10, 12, 14), put these sts on a thread; k2tog, work to last 6 (8, 10, 12, 14, 16) sts, k2togtbl, put remaining 4 (6, 8, 0, 12, 14) sts on a thread.
Row 2: P2togtbl, work to last 2 sts, p2tog.
Row 3: K2tog, work 26 (30, 34, 38, 42, 46), k2togtbl, turn. Put remaining sts on a stitch holder or thread.
Row 4: Work to last 2 sts, p2tog.
Row 5: K2tog, work to last 2 sts, k2togtbl.
Row 6: Work to last 2 sts, p2tog.
Rows 7 to 10: Repeat rows 5 and 6 twice more.
Row 11: Work to last 2 sts, k2togtbl.
Row 12: In pattern.
Repeat rows 11 and 12 five (six, seven, seven, seven, seven) times more.
Continue as follows:
Row 1: Work to last 2 sts, k2togtbl.
Rows 2 To 4: In pattern.
Repeat rows 1 to 4 until 10 (11, 12, 14, 16, 18) sts remain. Now work straight for the same total number of rows as for the back. Break yarn, and leave the sts on a thread or stitch holder for the shoulder.

55

Return to the 31 (35, 39, 43, 47, 51) sts for the right front. Put the next stitch (the centre front) on a thread or pin. Place the rest on the needle and work as follows:

Row 1: K2tog, work to last 2 sts, k2togtbl.
Row 2: P2tog, work to end of row.
Repeat rows 1 and 2 four times more. Continue as follows:
Row 11: K2tog, work to end of row.
Row 12: In pattern.
Repeat rows 11 and 12 five (six, seven, seven, seven, seven) times more. Continue as follows:
Row 1: K2tog, work to end of row.
Rows 2 To 4: In pattern.
Repeat rows 1 to 4 until 10 (11, 12, 14, 16, 18) sts remain. Now work straight for the same number of rows as for the back. Graft shoulders. Sew up side seams.

NECK BAND

With a thin needle, pick up and knit 46 (50, 54, 60, 66, 72) sts from the left side of the neck, PM, take the centre st from the pin and k1, pick up and knit 45 (49, 53, 59, 65, 71) sts from the right side of the neck, k25 (31, 37, 41, 45, 49) sts from the back neck. 117 (131, 145, 161, 177, 193) sts

Change to 4.5 mm circ or dpns, work as follows:
Round 1: *K1, p1. Repeat from * to 2 sts before the M, k2togtbl, SM, k1B, k2tog, *p1, k1. Repeat from * to last st, p1.
Round 2: *K1, p1. Repeat from * to 3 sts before the M, k1, p2tog, SM, k1B, p2tog, *k1, p1. Repeat from * to end of round.
Repeat rounds 1 and 2 twice more. Cast off in rib, decreasing each side of the centre front st as before.

ARM BANDS

Start at the seam under the arm. Take and knit 4 (6, 8, 10, 12, 14) sts from the thread, pick up and knit 90 (98, 104, 114, 124, 134) sts from the side of the arm-hole, take and knit 4 (6, 8, 10, 12, 14) sts from the other thread. 98 (110, 120, 134, 148, 162) sts.
Round 1: *K1, p1. Repeat from * to end of round.
Repeat round 1 five times more. Cast off in rib.

FINISHING

Weave in all ends. Wash and block.

CHARTS

CHART 1

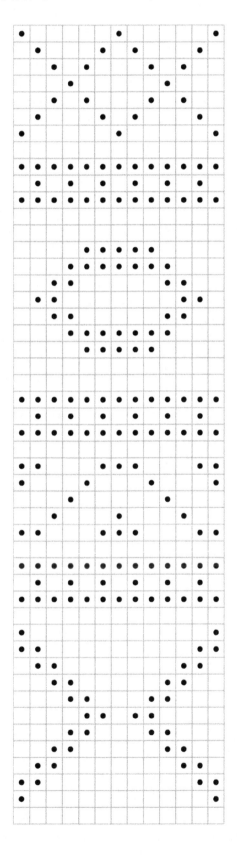

CHART 2

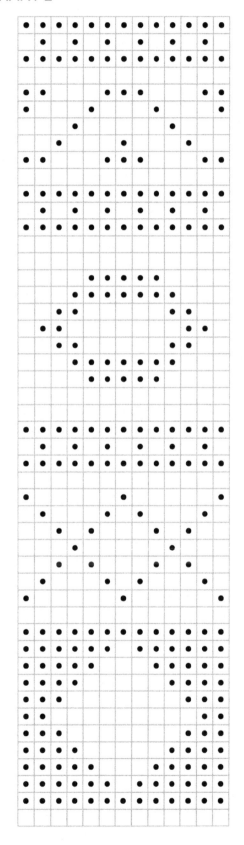

Braeland Sweater

A simple pattern with an ancient origin.

MATERIALS

300 (350, 400, 450, 500, 600, 700, 850, 1000) g aran weight yarn
pairs 4 and 5 mm (US 6 and 8) needles
circular 4 mm needle (length 60 cm)
6 stitch holders or lengths of yarn

SIZES

To fit chest: 24 (28, 32, 38, 42, 48, 52, 58, 64)"
Actual chest: 28 (33, 39, 44, 50, 55, 61, 66, 72)"
Length: 16 (18, 20, 22, 24, 26, 27, 28, 29)"
Sleeve: 15 (16, 17, 18, 19, 20, 21, 22, 23)"
Length and sleeve length are easily adjustable.

TENSION

17½ sts and 24 rows to 4" over pattern on larger needles after washing and blocking

PATTERN

BACK

On smaller needles, cast on 60 (72, 84, 96, 108, 120, 132, 144, 156) sts.
Work in k1, p1 rib for 2 (2½, 2½, 3, 3, 3, 3½, 3½, 3½)".
Next Row: P1, m1, p to end of row.

Change to larger needles.
Work the Braeland Chart, noting that the pattern has a 12 st repeat, and working the last stitch in row as first of pattern repeat.
Continue straight until work measures 10½ (12, 13½, 15, 16½, 18, 18, 18, 18)".
Adjust length here.

Next Row: Cast off 2 (2, 3, 4, 5, 6, 8, 10, 12) sts, pattern to end of row.
Next Row: As last row.

Work straight for a further 5½ (6, 6½, 7, 7½, 8, 9, 10, 11)".

Next Row: Work 17 (21, 25, 29, 32, 36, 39, 42, 45) and place on a holder for the right shoulder; work 23 (27, 29, 31, 35, 37, 39, 41, 43) and place on a holder for the back neck; work remaining sts and leave on holder for left shoulder.

FRONT

Work as back until work measures 4 (4, 4, 4, 4, 4½, 5, 6, 7)" from the start of the armhole.

Shape the neck
Row 1: Work 21 (25, 31, 35, 40, 44, 47, 52, 55), k2tog; turn. Place remaining sts on a stitch holder.
Row 2: P2tog, work to end of row.
Row 3: Work to last 2 sts, k2tog.
Repeat Rows 2 and 3 1 (2, 2, 2, 3, 3, 3, 4, 4) times more, then Row 2 again.
Work straight on remaining 17 (21, 25, 29, 32, 36, 39, 42, 45) sts until the front measures the same as the back. Leave sts on a holder.
Return to held sts. Place next 11 (15, 13, 15, 15, 17, 19, 17, 19) sts on a holder for the front neck.
Row 1: Ssk, work to end of row.
Row 2: Work to last 2 sts, p2togtbl.
Repeat Rows 1 and 2 3 (3, 4, 4, 5, 5, 5, 6, 6) times more.
Work straight on remaining 17 (21, 25, 29, 32, 36, 39, 42, 45) sts until the front measures the same as the back. Leave sts on a holder.

SLEEVES

On smaller needles, cast on 30 (36, 42, 42, 48, 48, 54, 54, 60) sts
Work in k1, p1 rib for 2 (2½, 2½, 3, 3, 3, 3½, 3½, 3½)".
Next Row: P1, m1, p to end of row.
Change to larger needles and work 6 (6, 6, 6, 6, 4, 4, 4, 4) rows for the chart for your size.
Shape sleeves as follows:
Row 1: k1, m1, work to last st, m1, k1.
Work 5 (5, 5, 5, 5, 3, 3, 3, 3) rows straight.
Repeat these 6 (6, 6, 6, 6, 4, 4, 4, 4) rows until there are 53 (57, 63, 69, 65, 83, 95, 79, 75) sts on the needle.
5th Size only: Work Rows 1 to 4 until there are 77 sts on the needle.

8th Size only: Work Rows 1 and 2 until there are 109 sts on the needle.
9th Size only: Work Rows 1 and 2 until there are 121 sts on the needle.

All Sizes
Work straight until the sleeve measures 15 (16, 17, 18, 19, 20, 21, 22, 23)".
Adjust length here.
Cast off.

NECK

Graft shoulders.
With the circular needles, and starting at the left shoulder, pick up and knit 12 (12, 16, 18, 20, 22, 22, 24, 26) sts down the left side front neck, knit the 11 (15, 13, 15, 15, 15, 17, 19, 17, 19) sts held from the front neck, pick up and knit 12 (12, 16, 18, 20, 22, 22, 24, 26) sts up the right side front neck, knit the 23 (27, 29, 31, 35, 37, 39, 41, 43) sts held from the back neck. 53 (57, 63, 69, 77, 83, 95, 109, 121) sts
Work in k1, p1 rib for 2 (2½, 2½, 3, 3, 3, 3½, 3½, 3½)".
Cast off loosely.

FINISHING

Sew up side seams and sleeve seams. Sew in sleeves, matching centre of sleeve to shoulder grafting and edges to marker row on front and back. Fold neck to wrong side. Sew cast off edge to first row of neck. Weave in all ends.

BRAELAND CHART

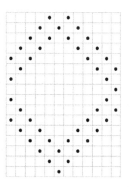

59

Quoyeden Sweater

A design inspired by Fair Isle patterns.

MATERIALS

300 (350, 350, 400, 450, 500, 550, 600, 700, 800, 900, 1000) g aran weight yarn
pairs 4 and 5 mm (US 6 and 8) needles
circular 4 mm needle (length 60 cm)
6 stitch holders or lengths of yarn

SIZES

To fit chest: 24 (28, 32, 36, 38, 42, 46, 50, 54, 56, 60, 64)"
Actual chest: 28 (32, 35, 39, 42½, 46, 49½, 53, 57, 60, 64, 67)"
Length: 16 (18, 20, 22, 24, 26, 27, 28, 29)"
Sleeve: 15 (16, 17, 18, 19, 20, 21, 22, 23)"
Length and sleeve length easily adjustable.

TENSION

18 sts and 24 rows to 4" over pattern on larger needles after washing and blocking.

BACK

On smaller needles, cast on 64 (72, 80, 88, 96, 104, 112, 120, 128, 136, 144, 152) sts.
Work in k1, p1 rib for 2 (2½, 2½, 2½, 3, 3, 3, 3, 3½, 3½, 3½, 3½)".
Next Row: P1, m1, p to end of row. 65 (73, 81, 89, 97, 105, 113, 121, 129, 137, 145, 153) sts
Change to larger needles. Work the Quoyeden Charts, noting that the pattern has an 8 st repeat.
Continue straight until work measures 10½ (12, 13, 14, 15, 16, 16½, 17, 18, 18, 18, 18)". *Adjust length here.*
Next Row: Cast off 2 (2, 3, 3, 4, 5, 6, 7, 8, 9, 10, 12) sts, pattern to end of row.

Next Row: As last row.
Work straight for a further 5½ (6, 6½, 7, 7, 7½, 8, 8½, 9, 9½, 10, 11)".
Next Row: Work 18 (21, 23, 26, 28, 30, 33, 35, 38, 40, 42, 43) and place on a holder for the right shoulder; work 25 (27, 29, 31, 33, 35, 35, 37, 37, 39, 41, 43) and place on a holder for the back neck; work remaining sts and leave on holder for left shoulder.

FRONT

Work as back until work measures 4 (4, 4, 4, 4, 4½, 4½, 5, 5, 5½, 6, 7)" from the start of the armhole.
Row 1: Work 22 (25, 29, 32, 34, 38, 41, 43, 48, 50, 52, 53), k2tog; turn. Place remaining sts on a stitch holder.
Row 2: P2tog, work to end of row.
Row 3: Work to last 2 sts, k2tog.
Repeat Rows 2 and 3 1 (1, 2, 2, 2, 3, 3, 3, 4, 4, 4, 4) times more, then Row 2 again.
Work straight on remaining 18 (21, 23, 26, 28, 30, 33, 35, 38, 40, 42, 43) sts until the front measures the same as the back. Leave sts on a holder.

Return to held sts. Place next 13 (15, 13, 15, 17, 15, 15, 17, 13, 15, 17, 19) sts on a holder for the front neck.
Row 1: Ssk, work to end of row.
Row 2: Work to last 2 sts, p2togtbl.
Repeat Rows 1 and 2 3 (3, 4, 4, 4, 5, 5, 5, 5, 6, 6, 6) times more.
Work straight on remaining 18 (21, 23, 26, 28, 30, 33, 35, 38, 40, 42, 43) sts until the front measures the same as the back. Leave sts on a holder.

SLEEVES

On smaller needles, cast on 32 (32, 40, 40, 40, 48, 48, 48, 56, 56, 56, 64) sts. Work in k1, p1 rib for 2 (2½, 2½, 2½, 3, 3, 3, 3, 3½, 3½, 3½, 3½)".

Next Row: P1, m1, p to end of row. 33 (33, 41, 41, 41, 49, 49, 49, 57, 57, 57, 65) sts

Change to larger needles and work 6 rows from the chart.

Shape sleeves as follows:

Row 1: K1, m1, work to last st, m1, k1. Work 5 rows straight.

Repeat these 6 rows until there are 53 (57, 63, 67, 69, 75, 69, 69, 77, 77, 77, 85) sts on the needle.

7th to 12th Sizes only:

Next Row: K1, m1, work to last st, m1, k1.

Work 3 rows straight.

Repeat these 4 rows until there are 83 (89, 95, 101, 109, 121) sts on the needle.

All Sizes:

Work straight until the sleeve measures 15 (16, 17, 17½ 18, 19, 19½, 20, 21, 21½, 22, 23)". *Adjust length here.* Cast off.

NECK

Graft shoulders.

With the circular needles, and starting at the left shoulder, pick up and knit 12 (12, 14, 16, 18, 18, 20, 22, 24, 24, 26, 26) sts down the left side front neck, knit the 13 (15, 13, 15, 17, 15, 15, 17, 13, 15, 17, 19) sts held from the front neck, pick up and knit 12 (12, 14, 16, 18, 18, 20, 22, 24, 24, 26, 26) sts up the right side front neck, knit the 25 (27, 29, 31, 33, 35, 35, 37, 37, 39, 41, 43) sts held from the back neck. 62 (66, 70, 78, 86, 86, 90, 98, 98, 102, 110, 114) sts

Work in k1, p1 rib for 2 (2½, 2½, 2½, 3, 3, 3, 3, 3½, 3½, 3½, 3½)". Cast off loosely.

FINISHING

Sew up side seams and sleeve seams. Sew in sleeves, matching centre of sleeve to shoulder grafting. Fold neck to wrong side. Sew cast off edge to first row of neck. Weave in all ends.

CHARTS

Work Chart 1, then Chart 2. Repeat as necessary.

CHART 1   CHART 2

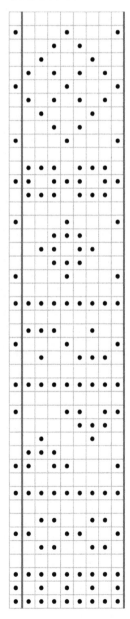

CHART FOR START OF SLEEVE

Use this chart to position the chart, then work through the main charts as required.

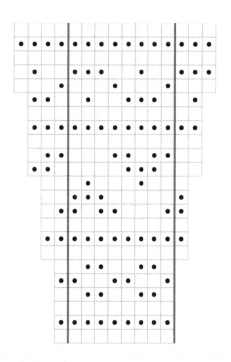

The original Quoyeden sweater, modelled here by Jill Strutt, went to Japan. It was bought by the producer of a film about the traditional knitwear of Scotland's Northern Isles.

Blanster Sweater

A fisherman's design typical of those found in the North of Scotland.

MATERIALS
300 (350, 400, 450, 500, 600, 700,
850, 1000) g aran weight yarn
pairs 4 and 5mm (US 6 and 8)
needles
circular 4 mm needle
6 stitch holders or lengths of yarn

SIZES
To fit chest: 24 (28, 32, 38, 42,
48, 52, 58, 64)"
Actual chest: 28 (33, 39, 44, 50,
55, 61, 66, 72)"
Length: 16 (18, 20, 22, 24, 26, 27,
28, 29)"
Sleeve: 15 (16, 17, 18, 19, 20, 21,
22, 23)"
*Length and sleeve length easily
adjustable.*

TENSION

17½ sts and 24 rows to 4" over
pattern on larger needles after
washing and blocking

BACK
On smaller needles, cast on 60 (72, 84, 96, 108, 120, 132, 144, 156) sts.
Work in k1, p1 rib for 2 (2½, 2½, 3, 3, 3, 3½, 3½, 3½)".
Next Row: P1, m1, p to end of row.

Change to larger needles.
Work the Blanster Chart, noting that the pattern has a 12 st repeat, and working the
last stitch in row as first of pattern repeat.

Continue straight until work measures 10½ (12, 13½, 15, 16½, 18, 18, 18, 18)".
Adjust length here.

Next Row: Cast off 2 (2, 3, 4, 5, 6, 8, 10, 12) sts, pattern to end of row.
Next Row: As last row.

Work straight for a further 5½ (6, 6½, 7, 7½, 8, 9, 10, 11)".
Next Row: Work 17 (21, 25, 29, 32, 36, 39, 42, 45) and place on a holder for the right shoulder; work 23 (27, 29, 31, 35, 37, 39, 41, 43) and place on a holder for the back neck; work remaining sts and leave on holder for left shoulder.

FRONT

Work as back until work measures 4 (4, 4, 4, 4, 4½, 5, 6, 7)" from the start of the armhole.
Row 1: Work 21 (25, 31, 35, 40, 44, 47, 52, 55), k2tog; turn. Place remaining sts on a stitch holder.
Row 2: P2tog, work to end of row.
Row 3: Work to last 2 sts, k2tog.
Repeat Rows 2 and 3 1 (2, 2, 2, 3, 3, 3, 4, 4) times more, then Row 2 again.
Work straight on remaining 17 (19, 25, 29, 32, 36, 39, 42, 45) sts until the front measures the same as the back. Leave sts on a holder.
Return to held sts. Place next 11 (15, 13, 15, 15, 17, 19, 17, 19) sts on a holder for the front neck.
Row 1: Ssk, work to end of row.
Row 2: Work to last 2 sts, p2togtbl.
Repeat Rows 1 and 2 2 (2, 3, 3, 4, 4, 4, 5, 5) times more.
Work straight on remaining 17 (21, 25, 29, 32, 36, 39, 42, 45) sts until the front measures the same as the back. Leave sts on a holder.

SLEEVES

On smaller needles, cast on 30 (36, 42, 42, 48, 48, 54, 54, 60) sts.
Work in k1, p1 rib for 2 (2½, 2½, 3, 3, 3, 3½, 3½, 3½)".

Next Row: P1, m1, p to end of row.
Change to larger needles and work 6 (6, 6, 6, 6, 4, 4, 4, 4) rows for the chart for your size.
Shape sleeves as follows:
Row 1: k1, m1, work to last st, m1, k1.
Work 5 (5, 5, 5, 5, 3, 3, 3, 3) rows straight.
Repeat these 6 (6, 6, 6, 6, 4, 4, 4, 4) rows until there are 53 (57, 63, 69, 65, 83, 95, 79, 75) sts on the needle.
5th Size only: Work Rows 1 to 4 until there are 77 sts on the needle.
8th Size only: Work Rows 1 and 2 until there are 109 sts on the needle.
9th Size only: Work Rows 1 and 2 until there are 121 sts on the needle.

All Sizes
Work straight until the sleeve measures 15 (16, 17, 18, 19, 20, 21, 22, 23)".
Adjust length here.
Cast off.

NECK

Graft shoulders.
With the circular needles, and starting at the left shoulder, pick up and knit 12 (12, 16, 18, 20, 22, 22, 24, 26) sts down the left side front neck, knit the 11 (15, 13, 15, 15, 15, 17, 19, 17, 19) sts held from the front neck, pick up and knit 12 (12, 16, 18, 20, 22, 22, 24, 26) sts up the right side front neck, knit the 23 (27, 29, 31, 35, 37, 39, 41, 43) sts held from the back neck. 58 (66, 74, 82, 90, 98, 102, 106, 114) sts
Work in k1, p1 rib for 2 (2½, 2½, 3, 3, 3, 3½, 3½, 3½)".
Cast off loosely.

FINISHING

Sew up side seams and sleeve seams. Sew in sleeves, matching centre of sleeve to shoulder grafting. Fold neck to wrong side. Sew cast off edge to first row of neck. Weave in all ends.

CHARTS

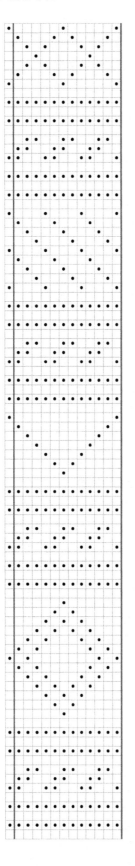

CHARTS FOR START OF SLEEVE
Use these charts to place the pattern centrally at the start of the sleeves.

SIZES 1, 3 and 4

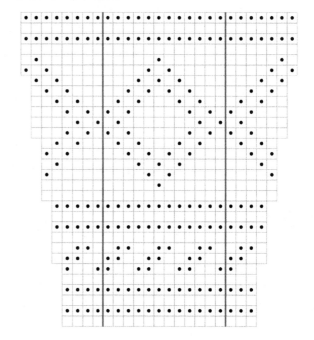

SIZES 2 and 5

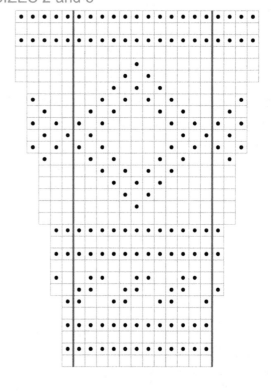

SIZES 6 and 9

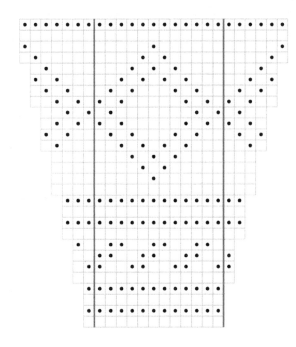

SIZES 7 and 8

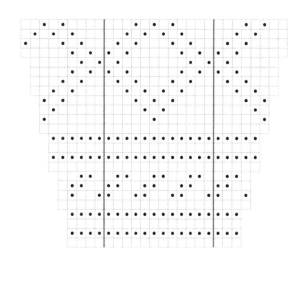

The original Blanster 20 years on, complete with coffee stains, but wearing well.

Braeland Hat

MATERIALS
60 (75, 80, 95, 115, 130) g
aran weight yarn
pair 5 mm (US 8) needles

SIZES
To fit: toddler (child, teen,
woman, man)
Unstretched circumference:
13 (16, 18½, 21, 24)"

TENSION
18 sts and 24 rows to 4"
over pattern after washing
and blocking

PATTERN

Cast on 60 (72, 84, 96, 108) sts.
Work in k1, p1 rib for 16 (22, 28, 32, 34)
rows.

Work the Braeland Hat Chart for 17 (23,
27, 31, 33) rows.
Purl 1 row.
Shape top as follows:
Row 1: *K4, k2tog. Repeat from * to end
of row.
Row 2 and all alternate rows: P.
Row 3: *K3, k2tog. Repeat from * to end
of row.
Row 5: *K2, k2tog. Repeat from * to end
of row.
Row 7: *K1, k2tog. Repeat from * to end
of row.
Row 9: *K2tog. Repeat from * to end of
row.

FINISHING
Draw sts up tightly and secure. Sew up
seam, reversing the seam on the brim.

BRAELAND HAT CHART

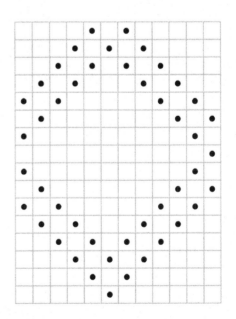

Quoyeden Hat

60 (75, 80, 95, 115, 130) g aran weight yarn
pair 5 mm (US 8) needles

To fit: toddler (child, teen, woman, man)
Unstretched circumference: 14 (16, 18, 21, 23)"

18 sts and 24 rows to 4" over pattern on larger needles after washing and blocking.

PATTERN

Cast on 64 (72, 80, 88, 96, 104) sts.
Work in k1, p1 rib for 16 (22, 28, 32, 34) rows.
Work the Quoyeden Hat Chart for your size.

Shape top as follows:
Row 1: *K6, k2tog. Repeat from * to end of row.
Row 2 and all alternate rows: P.
Row 3: *K5, k2tog. Repeat from * to end of row.
Row 5: *K4, k2tog. Repeat from * to end of row.
Row 7: *K3, k2tog. Repeat from * to end of row.
Row 9: *K2, k2tog. Repeat from * to end of row.
Row 11: *K1, k2tog. Repeat from * to end of row.
Row 12: *P2tog. Repeat from * to end of row.

Draw sts up tightly, and sew up seam, reversing the seam on the ribbing.

THE CHARTS

CHART FOR 1st SIZE

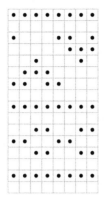

CHART FOR 2nd SIZE

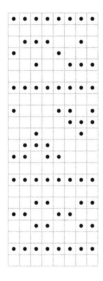

CHART FOR 3rd SIZE

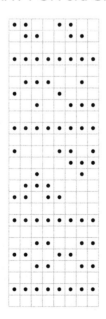

CHART FOR 4th SIZE

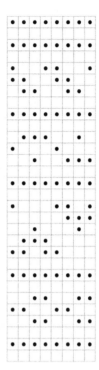

CHART FOR 5th SIZE

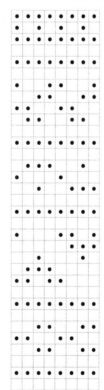

Blanster Hat

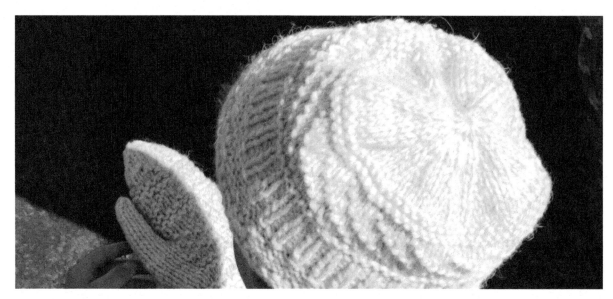

MATERIALS
60 (75, 80, 95, 115, 130) g aran weight yarn
pair 5 mm (US 8) needles

SIZES
To fit toddler: (child, teen, woman, man)
Unstretched circumference: 13 (16, 18½, 21, 24)"

TENSION
18 sts and 24 rows to 4" over pattern on larger needles after washing and blocking

PATTERN

Cast on 60 (72, 84, 96, 108) sts.
Work through the Brim Chart for your size.
Work 7 (9, 11, 13, 13) rows in k1, p1 rib. The right side of the brim is now the wrong side of the hat (as it will be turned up in wear).
Starting with a knit row, work 4 rows in stocking stitch.
Work through the Main Chart for your size.

Shape top as follows:
Row 1: *K4, k2tog. Repeat from * to end of row.
Row 2 and all alternate rows: P.
Row 3: *K3, k2tog. Repeat from * to end of row.
Row 5: *K2, k2tog. Repeat from * to end of row.
Row 7: *K1, k2tog. Repeat from * to end of row.
Row 9: *K2tog. Repeat from * to end of row.

FINISHING
Draw sts up tightly and secure. Sew up seam, reversing the seam on the brim.

CHARTS

BRIM CHART 1st SIZE

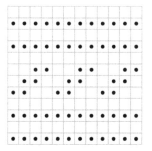

BRIM CHART 2nd SIZE

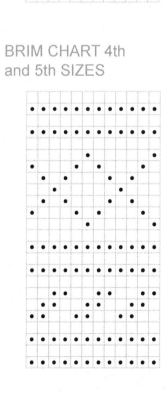

MAIN CHART 1st SIZE

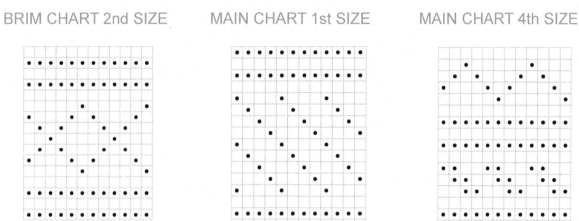

MAIN CHART 4th SIZE

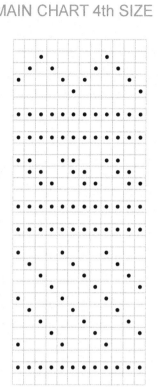

BRIM CHART 3rd SIZE

MAIN CHART 2nd SIZE

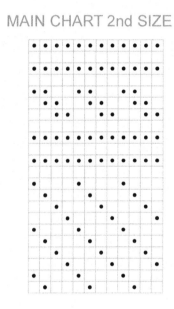

MAIN CHART 5th SIZE

BRIM CHART 4th
and 5th SIZES

MAIN CHART 3rd SIZE

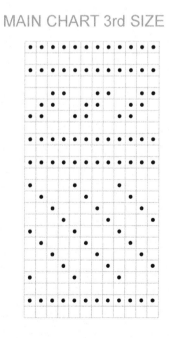

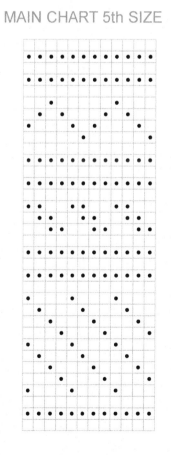

Braeland Mittens

MATERIALS
50 (60, 75, 100, 125) g aran weight yarn
pair 5 mm needles
2 stitch markers

SIZE

To fit: child (teen, woman, man, large man)
Palm circumference: 5½ (6½, 8, 8, 9½)"
Length of hand: 5 (6, 7½, 8½, 10)"

TENSION

17½ sts and 24 rows to 4" over pattern after washing and blocking

PATTERN

CUFF

Cast on 24 (30, 36, 36, 42) sts.
Work in k1, p1 rib for 8 (10, 12, 14, 16) rows or desired length of cuff.
Next Row: P1, m1, p to end of row. 25 (31, 37, 37, 43) sts

Thumb Gusset

Work from the chart as follows, repeating it as required:
Row 1: Work 12 (15, 18, 18, 21), PM, m1, PM, work to end of row.
Row 2: Work 12 (15, 18, 18, 21), SM, p1, SM, work to end of row.
Row 3: Work to M, SM, m1, k to M, m1, SM, work to end of row.
Row 4: Work to M, SM, p to M, SM, work to end of row.
Row 5: Work to M, SM, k to M, SM, work to end of row.
Row 6: As Row 4.
Repeat Rows 3 to 6 until there are 9 (11, 13, 13, 15) sts between the markers, finishing after a 6th row.

THUMB

Next Row: Work to M, SM, k to M, RM, turn.
Next Row: P to M. RM, turn.
Work 8 (10, 10, 12,14) more rows on these sts.
Next Row: K2tog to last st, k1.
Break off yarn, and thread through remaining sts. Sew up thumb.

HAND

With RSF rejoin yarn at base of the thumb. Work to end of row.
Continue working from the chart across all sts for a further 15 (19, 23, 27, 33) rows. *Adjust length here.*

Shape top
Row 1: *K2tog, k4. Repeat from * to end of row.
Row 2: *P3, p2tog. Repeat from * to end of row.
Row 3: *K2tog, k2. Repeat from * to end of row.
Row 4: *P1, p2tog. Repeat from * to end of row.
Row 5: *K2tog. Repeat from * to end of row.
Break off yarn, and thread through remaining sts.

FINISHING
Sew up side seam. Weave in all ends.

CHART

Quoyeden and Blanster Mittens

*These two pairs of mittens share the same stitch numbers,
but use different charts.*

MATERIALS
50 (60, 75, 100, 125) g aran weight yarn
pair 5 mm needles
2 stitch markers

SIZE
To fit: child (teen, woman, small man, man)
Palm circumference: 5½ (6½, 8, 8, 9½)"
Length of hand: 5 (6, 7½, 8½, 10)"

TENSION
17½ sts and 24 rows to 4" over pattern

CUFF
Cast on 24 (28, 32, 36, 40) sts.
Work in k1, p1 rib for 8 (10, 12, 14, 16) rows or desired length of cuff.

Thumb Gusset
Work from the chart as follows, repeating it as required:
Row 1: Work 12 (14, 16, 18, 20), PM, m1, PM, work to end of row.
Row 2: Work 12 (15, 18, 18, 20), SM, p1, SM, work to end of row.
Row 3: Work to M, SM, m1, k to M, m1, SM, work to end of row.
Row 4: Work to M, SM, p to M, SM, work to end of row.
Row 5: Work to M, SM, k to M, SM, work to end of row.
Row 6: As Row 4.
Repeat Rows 3 to 6 until there are 7, (9, 11, 13, 15) sts between the markers, finishing after Row 6.

THUMB

Next Row: Work to M, SM, k to M, RM, turn.

Next Row: P to M. RM, turn.

Work 8 (10, 10, 12,14) more rows on these sts.

Next Row: K2tog to last st, k1.

Break off yarn, and thread through remaining sts. Sew up thumb.

HAND

With RSF rejoin yarn at base of the thumb. Work to end of row.

Continue working from the chart across all sts for a further 15 (19, 23, 27, 33) rows. *Adjust length here.*

Shape top

Row 1: *K2, k2tog. Repeat from * to end of row.

Row 2: P.

Row 3: *K1, k2tog. Repeat from * to end of row.

Row 4: P.

Row 5: *K2tog. Repeat from * to end of row.

Break off yarn, and thread through remaining sts.

FINISHING

Sew up side seam. Weave in all ends.

CHARTS

QUOYEDEN CHART

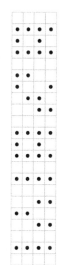

BLANSTER CHART

Braeland, Quoyeden and Blanster Scarves

*All three scarves use the same number of stitches,
but use different stitch patterns.*

MATERIALS

For each scarf:
300 g aran weight yarn
pair 6 mm (US 10) needles
crochet hook for knotting fringe

SIZE

8" wide and 60" long excluding fringe

Note - allow about 50 g yarn per 12" scarf
and 50 g for the fringing

TENSION

16 st to 4" over pattern after washing and
blocking. The row tension differs
between patterns and sections of the
patterns.

PATTERN

With 6 mm needles cast on 31 sts loosely. Knit 5 rows.
Now work from your choice of chart for
about 59" or desired length, finishing with
the right side facing.
Knit 5 rows. Cast off loosely.

FINISHING
Weave in all ends.

FRINGING

Cut 64 lengths of wool about 16" long.
Take 2 lengths of yarn, and knot them
through the first and alternate stitches of
the cast on and cast off ends.

CHARTS

BRAELAND SCARF CHART

QUOYEDEN SCARF CHART   BLANSTER SCARF CHART

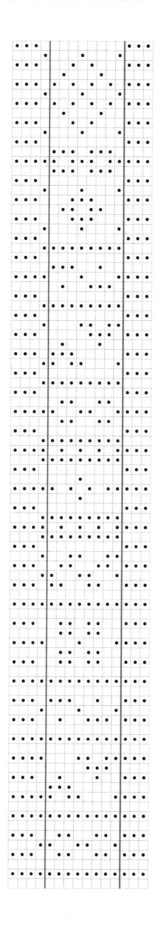
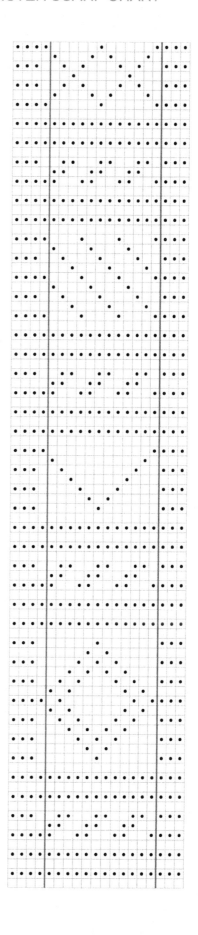

Cat's Paw Cropped Top

Pretty, versatile and warm. Perfect for any occasion.

MATERIALS
100 (120, 150, 180) g fine North Ronaldsay yarn
pair 6 mm (US 10) needles
8 (12, 12, 16) button about 20 mm diameter if desired

SIZE
To fit: child (teen, woman, plus)
Width: 23 (27, 31, 35)"
Back length: 12 (13½, 15, 16½)"
Front length: 9 (10½, 12, 13½)"
Lengths easily adjustable.

TENSION
14 sts and 24 rows to 4" over pattern

BACK
Cast on 83 (97, 111, 125) sts.
Rows 1 to 3: S1p, k to end of row.
Work through the chart 8 (9, 10, 11) times.
Adjust back length here.

Neck
Keeping the pattern correct, continue as follows:
Rows 1 to 4: Work 38 (45, 52, 59) k7, work to end of row.
Row 5: Work 38 (45, 52, 59), k4; turn. Place remaining sts on a holder.
Row 6: S1p, k3, work to end of row.
Continue on these sts only until 6 (7, 8, 9) repeats have been worked, then work Rows 1 to 5 of the chart again, finishing at the neck edge.
Break yarn and leave sts on a holder. Return to held sts.
With RSF, rejoin yarn to neck edge.
Row 1: S1p, k2, work to end of row.
Row 2: Work to last 3 sts, k3.
Continue until 6 (7, 8, 9) repeats have been worked, then work Rows 1 to 5 of the chart again.
Next Row: Work 38 (45, 52, 59), k3, place the other sts on the needle, k4, work to end of row.

FRONT
Rows 1 to 4: Work 38 (45, 52, 59), k7, work to end of row.
Row 5: Work 83 (97, 111, 125).
Continue in pattern over all sts until 5 (6, 7, 8) repeats have been worked since the neck. *Adjust front length here.*
Next Row: S1p, k to end of row.
Repeat this row twice more. Cast off loosely.

FINISHING
Weave in all ends. Wash and block. If desired, sew 4 (6, 6, 8) pairs of buttons together and use to join the front and back under the arms.

CAT'S PAW CHART

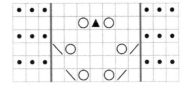

Row 1: K3, *k1, k2tog, yo, k1, yo, ssk, k1. Repeat from * to last 3 sts, k3.
Row 2 and all even numbered rows: K3, p to last 3 sts, k3.
Row 3: K3, *k2tog, yo, k3, yo, ssk. Repeat from * to last 3 sts, k3.
Row 5: K3, *k2, yo, k3togtbl, yo, k2. Repeat from * to last 3 sts, k3.

Cabled Scarf

Perfect for tucking into the collar of a coat.

MATERIALS
250g aran weight yarn
pair 5.5 mm (US 9) needles

MEASUREMENTS
7½" wide and 56" long
Length easily adjustable.

TENSION
20 sts and 24 rows to 4" over pattern
after washing and blocking

PATTERN

With 5.5 mm needles cast on 35 sts.
Rows 1 to 3: P1, *k1, p1. Repeat from
* to the end of the row.
Row 4: (P1, k1) three times, m1, (p1,
k1) six times, m1, (p1, k1) five times,
m1, (p1, k1) three times, p1. 38 sts

Now work from the chart, noting that the
pattern has a 12 row repeat, until the
work measures 55" or about 1" less than
the required length, finishing after a 6th
row.

Continue as follows:
Row 1: (P1, k1) twice, p1, k2tog, (p1,
k1) five times, p1, k2tog, (p1, k1) five
times, p1, k2tog, (p1, k1) twice, p1.
Rows 2 and 3: P1, *k1, p1. Repeat
from * to the end of the row.
Row 4: Cast off in pattern.

FINISHING
Weave in ends. Wash the scarf pinning
to dry.

CHART

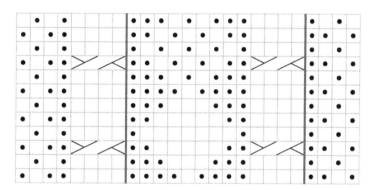

Row 1: P1, k1, p2, *k4, p4, k1, p4. Repeat from * once, k4, p2, k1, p1.
Row 2: (P1, k1) twice, p4, *k3, p3, k3, p4. Repeat from * once, (k1, p1) twice.
Row 3: P1, k1, p2, *C4B, p2, k5, p2. Repeat from * once, C4B, p2, k1, p1.
Row 4: (P1, k1) twice, p4, *k1, p7, k1, p4. Repeat from * once, (k1, p1) twice.
Row 5: P1, k1, p2, *k4, p2, k5, p2. Repeat from * once, k4, p2, k1, p1.
Row 6: As Row 2.
Row 7: As Row 1.
Row 8: (P1, k1) twice, p4, *k3, p1, k1, p1, k3, p4. Repeat from * once, (k1, p1) twice.
Row 9: P1, k1, p2, *C4B, p2, (k1, p1) twice, k1, p2. Repeat from * once, C4B, p2,
k1, p1.
Row 10: (P1, k1) twice, p4, *(k1, p1) four times, k1, p4. Repeat from * once, (k1, p1)
twice.
Row 11: P1, k1, p2, *k4, p2, (k1, p1) twice, k1, p2. Repeat from * once, k4, p2, k1,
p1.
Row 12: As Row 8.

Child's Vest

Light and warm, and suitable for boys and girls of all ages.

MATERIALS

80 (100, 120, 140, 170, 200, 240, 280, 320) g aran weight yarn
pairs 3 and 3.5 mm (US 3 and 4) needles

SIZE

To fit chest: 20 (22, 24, 27, 29, 31, 34, 36, 39)"
Actual chest: 21 (23½, 26, 29, 31½, 34, 36½, 39, 41½)"
Length: 14 (16, 18, 20, 21, 22, 23, 24, 25)" *Length easily adjustable.*

TENSION

28 sts and 32 rows to 4" over pattern on larger needles

BACK

With smaller needles, cast on 74 (84, 92, 102, 110, 120, 128, 138, 146) sts. Work 9 (11,13, 13, 15, 15, 17, 17, 17) rows in k1, p1 rib.
Next Row: K1, m1 (0, 1, 0, 1, 0, 1, 0, 1) rib to end of row. 75 (84, 93, 102, 111, 120, 129, 138, 147) sts
Change to larger needles and work from the chart until the piece measures 9 (10½, 12, 13, 13½, 14, 14½, 15, 15)" *Adjust length here.*
Keeping the pattern correct, decrease for the armholes as follows:
Rows 1 and 2: Cast off 4 (4, 5, 6, 7, 9, 11, 13, 15) sts, patt to end of row.
Row 3: K2tog, patt to last 2 sts, ssk.
Row 4: In patt.
Repeat Rows 3 and 4 3 (3, 3, 4, 5, 6, 7, 8, 9) times more. 59 (68, 75, 80, 85, 88, 89, 94, 97) sts
Work straight until the piece measures 5 (5½, 6, 7, 7½, 8, 8½, 9, 10)" from the start of the armhole shaping.

Next Row: Cast off 15 (18 (21, 24, 25, 26, 26, 27, 28), patt to last 15 (18, 21, 24, 25, 26, 26, 27, 28) sts, cast off these sts. Place remaining 29 (32, 33, 34, 35, 36, 37, 39, 41) sts on a stitch holder.

FRONT

Work as for the Back to the start of the armhole shaping.
Keeping the pattern correct, decrease for the neck and armholes as follows:
Rows 1 and 2: Cast off 4 (4, 5, 6, 7, 9, 11, 13, 15) sts, patt to end of row.
Row 3: K2tog, patt 31 (35, 39, 42, 41, 48, 51, 53, 61) for the left front, turn.
Place next 1 (2, 1, 2, 1, 2, 1, 2, 1) sts on a stitch holder, and remaining 33 (37, 41, 43, 42, 50, 53, 55, 63) sts on a thread for the right front.
Continue with the left front.
Row 4: P2tog, patt to end of row.
Row 5: K2tog, patt to last 2 sts, ssk.
Row 6: In patt.
Repeat Rows 5 and 6 2 (2, 2, 3, 4, 5, 6, 7, 8) times more. This completes the armhole shaping.
Continue shaping the necks as follows:
Row 1: Patt to last 2 sts, ssk.
Rows 2 to 4: In patt.
Repeat Rows 1 to 4 until 15 (18, 21, 24, 25, 26, 26, 27, 28) sts remain.
Work straight until the armhole measures the same as the Back.
Cast off.
Return to the held sts and with RSF, continue as follows:
Row 1: Patt to last 2 sts, ssk.
Row 2: Patt to last 2 sts, p2togtbl.
Row 3: K2tog, patt to last 2 sts, ssk.
Row 4: In patt.

Repeat Rows 3 and 4 2 (2, 2, 3, 4, 5, 6, 7, 8) times more. This completes the armhole shaping.
Continue shaping the necks as follows:
Row 1: K2tog, patt to end of row.
Rows 2 to 4: In patt.
Repeat Rows 1 to 4 until 15 (18, 21, 24, 25, 26, 26, 27, 28) sts remain.
Work straight until the armhole measures the same as the back.
Cast off.

NECK

Join the right shoulder.
With RSF and smaller needles, pick up and knit 40 (44, 48, 56, 60, 64, 68, 72, 80) sts down the left front neck, PM, work the sts from the pin as k1 (k2tog, k1, k2tog, k1, k2tog, k1, k2tog, k1), pick up and knit 40 (44, 48, 56, 60, 64, 68, 72, 80) sts up the right front neck, k27 (32, 31, 34, 33, 36, 35, 37, 39), k2tog 1(0, 1, 0, 1, 0, 1, 1, 1) times. 109 (121, 129, 147, 155, 165, 173, 173, 201) sts

Row 1: [K1, p1] to 4 sts before M, k1, p2tog, p1b, SM, p2tog, [k1, p1] to end of row.
Row 2: [K1, p1] to 3 sts before M, k1, p2tog, SM, k1b, p2tog, [k1, p1] to end of row.
Repeat Rows 1 and 2 2 (2, 2, 2, 3, 3, 4, 4, 5, 5) more. Cast off in rib, decreasing as before.
Join left shoulder.

ARMHOLES

With RSF and smaller needles, pick up and knit 78 (84, 88, 92, 104, 118, 130, 142, 152, 170) sts round the armhole,
Row 1: *K1, p1. Repeat from * to end of row.
Repeat this row 4 (4, 5, 5, 5, 6, 6, 7, 7) times more. Cast off in rib.

FINISHING

Sew neck, side and armhole seams.
Weave in ends. Wash and block.

CHART

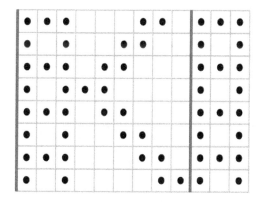

Striped Triangular Shawl
by Elly Doyle

This shawl is simple to make, with bands of stocking stitch and garter stitch. The bold lines are finished off with a pretty picot cast-off.

MATERIALS

2 x 100 g North Ronaldsay fine yarn

5 mm needles or size to achieve tension

1 stitch marker

Sample shows a plain version and marled version of the same colour.

SIZE

67½" wide and 33½" deep

TENSION

13 sts and 28 rows to 4" over stocking stitch after washing and blocking

CONSTRUCTION

The shawl is worked flat, outwards from the centre top of the spine.

STOCKING STITCH PATTERN

Row 1 (RS): K3, yo, k to M, yo, SM, k1, yo, k until 3 sts remain, yo, k3.

Row 2: K3, p until 3 sts remain, k3.

GARTER STITCH PATTERN

Row 1 (RS): K3, yo, k to M, yo, SM, k1, yo, k until 3 sts remain, yo, k3.

Row 2: K.

PICOT CAST-OFF

*Using cable cast-on method, cast on 2 sts. Cast off 4 sts. Repeat from * until all sts are cast off.

PATTERN

Using plain yarn, cast on 9 sts.

Next row: K3, yo, k1, yo, PM, k1, yo, k1, yo, k3.

Next row: K3, p until 3 sts remain, k3.

Work 19 repeats of Stocking Stitch Pattern.

Using marled yarn, work 5 repeats of Garter Stitch Pattern.

Using plain yarn, work 15 repeats of Stocking Stitch Pattern.

Using marled yarn, work 5 repeats of Garter Stitch Pattern.

Using plain yarn, work 10 repeats of Stocking Stitch Pattern.

Using marled yarn, work 5 repeats of Garter Stitch Pattern.

Using plain yarn, work 5 repeats of Stocking Stitch Pattern.

Using marled yarn, work 5 repeats of Garter Stitch Pattern.

Using plain yarn, work the Picot Cast-Off.

FINISHING

Weave in all ends. Wash and dry flat, pulling to shape.

Skinny Crescent Shawl

by Elly Doyle

Long enough to wrap round your neck a couple of times, or to knot as a collar, this shawl will be useful in all seasons.

MATERIALS

100 g North Ronaldsay fine yarn

5 mm needles or size to achieve tension

smaller needle to pick up sts

SIZE

69½" wide and 7" deep

TENSION

13 sts and 28 rows to 4" over stocking stitch after washing and blocking

CONSTRUCTION

The edging is worked first and stitches picked up for the centre, which is worked using short rows.

PATTERN

EDGING

Cast on 5 sts and work through the first 16 rows of the chart, then repeat Rows 17 to 36 twenty-four times and then Rows 37 to 50. Leave remaining 5 sts on needle.

CENTRE

Using smaller needle, pick up 1 st for every 2 rows, then pick up 5 sts from cast-on edge. Using larger needle, knit the 5 sts from the tip, then knit the picked up stitches. 265 sts

Next Row: Knit 153, turn.

Next Row: Knit 41, turn.

Next Row: Knit to st before gap, k2tog, k3, turn.

Repeat this row 17 times more.

Next Row: Knit to st before gap, k2tog, k8, turn.

Repeat this row 9 times more.

Next Row: Knit to end of row.

Repeat this row 3 times more.

Cast off loosely.

FINISHING

Sew in ends. Wash and block flat, pinning out the points.

CHART

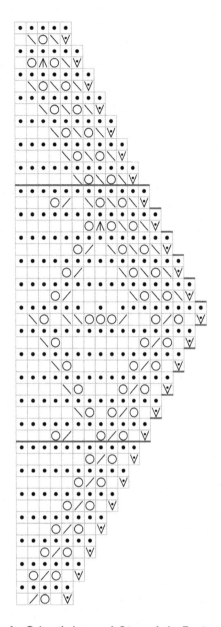

Row 1: S1p, k1, yo, k2tog, k1. 5 sts

Rows 2 and all alternate rows except Row 28: K.

Row 3: S1p, k1, yo, k2tog, yo, k1. 6 sts

Row 5: S1p, k1, yo, k2tog, yo, k2. 7 sts

Row 7: S1p, k1, yo, k2tog, yo, k3. 8 sts

Row 9: S1p, k1, yo, k2tog, yo, k4. 9 sts

Row 11: S1p, k1, yo, k2tog, yo, k5. 10 sts

Row 13: S1p, k1, yo, k2tog, yo, k6. 11 sts

Row 17: 1p, k1, yo, k2tog, yo, k1, yo, ssk, k5. 13 sts

Row 19: S1p, k1, yo, k2tog, yo, k3, yo, ssk, k4. 14 sts

Row 21: S1p, k1, yo, k2tog, yo, k5, yo, ssk, k3. 15 sts

Row 23: S1p, k1, yo, k2tog, yo, k7, yo, ssk, k2. 16 sts

Row 25: S1p, k1, yo, k2tog, yo, k2, k2tog, yo three times, ssk twice, k1, yo, ssk, k1. 17 sts

Row 26: K6, p1, k1, p1, k8.

Row 27: S1p,[ssk, yo] twice, ssk, k5, k2tog, yo, k3. 16 sts

Row 28: K6, p1, k1, p1, k8.

Row 29: S1p, [ssk, yo] twice, ssk, k3, k2tog, yo, k4. 15 sts

Row 31: S1p, [ssk, yo] twice, ssk, k1, k2tog, yo, k5. 14 sts

Row 33: S1p, [ssk, yo] twice, k3togtbl, yo, k6. 13 sts

Row 35: S1p, [ssk, yo] twice, ssk, k1, k2tog, yo, k3. 12 sts

Repeat Rows 17 to 36 twenty-three times more.

Row 37: S1p, [ssk, yo] twice, ssk, k5. 11 sts

Row 39: S1p, [ssk, yo] twice, ssk, k4. 10 sts

Row 41: S1p, ssk, yo twice, ssk, k3. 9 sts

Row 43: S1p, [ssk, yo] twice, ssk, k2. 8 sts

Row 45: S1p, [ssk, yo] twice, ssk, k1. 7 sts

Row 47: S1p, ssk, yo, k3togtbl, yo, k1. 6 sts

Row 49: S1p, ssk, yo, ssk, k1. 5 sts

Row 50: K.

Flower Shawl
by Elly Doyle

This pretty shawl is worked in one piece from the tip up,
so you can make it any size you want.

MATERIALS

100 g North Ronaldsay fine yarn

4 mm needles or size to achieve tension

smaller needle to pick up sts

SIZE

27" across the top and 15" deep

TENSION

18 sts and 36 rows to 4" over garter stitch after washing and blocking

CONSTRUCTION

The tip of the shawl is worked, then sts are picked up along the straight edge. Work proceeds upwards, increasing in width until desired size is reached.

Place markers where lines indicate, moving them back to 22 sts in from each side after reaching the end of a repeat.

This pattern requires you to pick up a few sts. For best results, I recommend picking up sts using the back leg of the stitch.

PATTERN

Cast on 3 sts. Work through the First Lace Repeat Chart.

Pick up and knit 6 sts from the twisted stitch edge onto the needle with the live stitches. Pick up and knit 3 sts from the cast-on edge onto the same needle.

Work the 19 rows of the Tip Chart.

Work the 12 rows of the Repeat Chart

seven times or until shawl is desired size. Work the Top Edge Chart, then cast off loosely.

FINISHING

Weave in loose ends. Wash and block, pinning out the lace points along the edge. When completely dry, remove pins and trim all yarn tails.

CHARTS

In all the Flouer charts an empty square is worked as a KNIT stitch on both odd and even rows. Note that some charts start with a WRONG SIDE row.

FIRST LACE REPEAT CHART

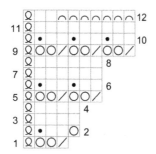

Row 3: K1tbl, k4.
Row 4: K4, k1tbl.
Row 5: K1tbl, [yo twice, k2tog] twice.
Row 6: [K2, p1] twice, k1tbl.
Row 7: K1tbl, k6.
Row 8: K6, k1tbl.
Row 9: K1tbl, [yo twice, k2tog] three times.
Row 10: [K2, p1] three times, k1tbl.
Row 11: K1tbl, k9.
Row 12: Cast off 7, k2, k1tbl.

Row 1 (WS): K1tbl, yo twice, k2tog.
Row 2 (RS): Yo, k2, k1, k1tbl.

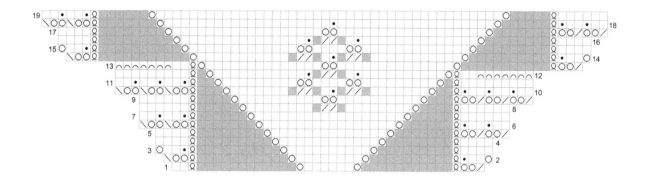

Row 1 (WS): P2, k1tbl, yo, k6, yo, k1tbl, yo twice, k2tog.
Row 2 (RS): Yo, k2, k1, k1tbl, yo, k8, yo, k1tbl, yo twice, ssk.
Row 3: Yo, k2, p1, k1tbl, yo, k10, yo, k1tbl, k4.
Row 4: K4, k1tbl, yo, k12, yo, k1tbl, k4.
Row 5: K4, k1tbl, yo, k14, yo, k1tbl, [yo twice, k2tog] twice.
Row 6: [K2, p1] twice, k1tbl, yo, k16, yo, k1tbl, [yo twice, ssk] twice.
Row 7: [K2, p1] twice, k1tbl, yo, k18, yo, k1tbl, k6.
Row 8: K6, k1tbl, yo, k8, k2tog twice, k8, yo, k1tbl, k6.
Row 9: K6, k1tbl, yo, k10, yo twice, k10, yo, k1tbl, [yo twice, k2tog] three times.
Row 10: [K2, k1] three times, k1tbl, yo, k7, k2tog twice, k1, p1, k2tog twice, k7, yo, k1tbl, [yo twice, ssk] three times.
Row 11: [K2, k1] three times, k1tbl, yo, k9, yo twice, k4, yo twice, k9, yo, k1tbl, k9.
Row 12: Cast off 7, k2, k1tbl, yo, k10, k1, p1, k2tog twice, p1, k11, yo, k1tbl, k9.
Row 13: Cast off 7, k2, k1tbl, yo, k14, yo twice, k14, yo, k1tbl, yo twice, k2tog.
Row 14: Yo, k2, p1, k1tbl, yo, k11, k2tog twice, k1, p1, k2tog twice, k11, yo, k1tbl, yo twice, ssk.
Row 15: Yo, k2, p1, k1tbl, yo, k13, yo twice, k4, yo twice, k13, yo, k1tbl, k4.
Row 16: K4, k1tbl, yo, k14, p1, k1, k2tog twice, p1, k15, yo, k1tbl, k4.
Row 17: P4, k1tbl, yo, k18, yo twice, k18, yo, k1tbl, [yo twice, k2tog] twice.
Row 18: [K2, p1] twice, k1tbl, yo, k19, p1, k20, yo, k1tbl, [yo twice, ssk] twice.
Row 19: [K2, p1] twice, k1tbl, yo, k42, yo, k1tbl, k6.

93

FLOUER REPEAT CHART

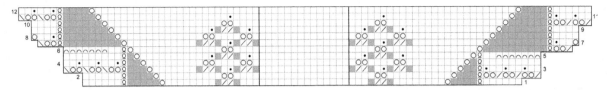

Row 1 (RS): K6, k1tbl, yo, k8, k2tog twice, k3, PM, k to 22 sts from end of row, PM, k3, k2tog twice, k8, yo, k1tbl, k6.

Row 2 (WS): K6, k1tbl, yo, k10, yo twice, k to 4 sts after 2nd M, yo twice, k10, yo, k1tbl, [yo twice, k2tog] three times.

Row 3: [K2, k1] three times, k1tbl, yo, k7, k2tog twice, p1, k1, k2tog twice, k to 2nd M, k2tog twice, k1, k, k2tog twice, k7, yo, k1tbl, (yo twice, ssk) three times.

Row 4: [K2, p1] three times, k1tbl, yo, k9, yo twice, k4, yo twice, k to 1 st after 2nd M, yo twice, k4, yo twice, k9, yo, k1tbl, k9.

Row 5: Cast off 7, k2, k1tbl, yo, k10, p1, k1, k2tog twice, p1, k to 1 st after 2nd M, p1, k1, k2tog twice, k1, k11, yo, k1tbl, k9.

Row 6: Cast off 7, k2, k1tbl, yo, k14, yo twice, k to 4 sts after 2nd M, yo twice, k14, yo, k1tbl, yo twice, k2tog.

Row 7: Yo, k2, p1, k1tbl, yo, k11, k2tog twice, p1, k1, k2tog twice, k to 2nd M, k2tog twice, k1, k, k2tog twice, k11, yo, k1tbl, yo twice, ssk.

Row 8: Yo, k2, k1, k1tbl, yo, k13, yo twice, k4, yo twice, k to 1 st after 2nd M, yo twice, k4, yo twice, k13, yo, k1tbl, k4.

Row 9: K4, k1tbl, yo, k14, p1, k1, k2tog twice, p1, k to 1 st after 2nd M, p1, k1, k2tog twice, k1, k15, yo, k1tbl, k4.

Row 10: K4, k1tbl, yo, k18, yo twice, k to 4 sts after 2nd M, yo twice, k18, yo, k1tbl, (yo twice, k2tog) twice.

Row 11: [K2, p1] twice, k1tbl, yo, k19, p1, k to 4 sts after 2nd M, p1, k20, yo, k1tbl, (yo twice, ssk) twice.

Row 12: [K2, p1] twice, k1tbl, yo, [k to M, RM] twice, k to last 7 sts, yo, k1tbl, k6.

FLOUER TOP EDGE CHART

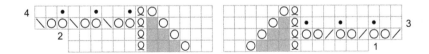

Row 1 (WS): K6, k1tbl, yo, k to last 7 sts, yo, k1tbl, k6.

Row 2 (RS): [K2tog, yo twice] three times, k1tbl, yo, k to last 7 sts, yo, k1tbl, k6.

Row 3: [K2tog, yo twice] three times, k1tbl, yo, k to last 10 sts, yo, k1tbl, [p1, k2] three times.

Row 4: K9, k1tbl, yo, k to last 10 sts, yo, k1tbl, [p1, k2] three times.

Fairnteckle Child's Sweater
by Elly Doyle

Shawl necked sweaters are so practical for children. They can get them on over their heads easily, but the neck keeps them warm! Elly has named this one from the Orkney word for a freckle.

MATERIALS
250 (300, 350, 400, 450) g aran weight yarn
4.5 and 5 mm (US 7 and 8) circular needles
spare 5 mm (US 8) needle
1 stitch marker
stitch holders or lengths of yarn
row counter

SIZES
To fit age: 2 (4, 6, 8, 10, 12) years
Garment chest: 23 (25, 27, 29, 31, 33)"
Length: 14 (15½, 17, 18½, 20, 22)"
Sleeve: 8½ (10½, 11½, 12½, 13½, 15)"
Length and sleeve length easily adjustable.

TENSION
16 sts and 24 rows to 4" on larger needles over Main Pattern Stitch after washing and blocking

CONSTRUCTION
The body is worked in the round until the underarm, then split and worked flat for the front and back. Sleeves are worked in the round and sewn into the armholes. The collar is picked up around the neckline and worked in garter stitch.

RIB PATTERN
Round 1: K1, p1.
Round 2: K.

MAIN PATTERN STITCH
Round 1: K1, p1, k2.
Round 2 & 4: K.
Round 3: K3, p1.

PATTERN

BODY
Using smaller needles, cast on 92 (100, 108, 116, 124, 132) sts. PM and join to work in the round. Work Rib Pattern for 6 (6, 8, 10, 12, 12) rounds.
Change to larger needles, work in Main Pattern Stitch until work measures 9 (10, 11, 12, 13, 14)" from cast-on edge.

Armhole shaping
Row 1: Cast off 2 (2, 3, 3, 3, 3), work 44 (48, 51, 55, 59, 63) sts in patt. Slip remaining 46 (50, 54, 58, 62, 66) sts to holder for Back; turn.
Row 2: Cast off 2 (2, 3, 3, 3, 3) sts, work to end of row. 42 (46, 48, 52, 56, 60) sts
Rows 3 and 4: Cast off 1 (2, 2, 2, 2, 3), patt to end of row.
Row 5: Cast off 1 (1, 1, 1, 2, 2), patt to end of row.
Row 6: Cast off 0 (0, 0, 0, 1, 1), patt to end of row.
Rows 7 and 8: Cast off 0 (0, 0, 0, 1, 1), patt to end of row. 38 (40, 42, 44, 46, 48) sts remain. This completes the armhole shaping.

Neck shaping
Next row: Work 12 (13, 13, 14, 15, 16) sts in patt, cast off 14 (14, 16, 16, 16, 16) sts for neck, patt to end of row.

RIGHT FRONT
On these 12 (13, 13, 14, 15, 16) sts, work in patt until work measures 5 (5.5, 6, 6.5, 7, 8)" from underarm splitting, noting number of row worked. Break yarn and slip stitches on to holder.

LEFT FRONT
Return to 12 (13, 13, 14, 15, 16) sts held for left front. Work the same number of rows as the Right Front. Break yarn and slip sts to holder.

BACK
Slip Back stitches from holder to larger needles.
Work underarm shaping as for the Front, then work in patt until Back is same length as Fronts to the shoulders.

Shoulder Seams
Turn work so WSF. Place Front Shoulder sts on a separate needle, and work a 3 needle cast off across shoulder sts, k14 (14, 16, 16, 16, 16) sts for back of neck, work 3 needle cast off across second shoulder. Turn so RSF.

COLLAR
Using smaller needle, pick up and knit 16 (18, 20, 20, 22, 26) sts up the right front neck, PM, k 14 (14, 16, 16, 16, 16) from back neck, PM, pick up and k 16 (18, 20, 20, 22, 26) sts down the left front neck.
Next row: Using larger needle, k to M, RM, [kfb, k1] to M, RM, k to end.
Work in garter stitch until length of collar is equal to the width of the cast off sts for front of Neck. Cast off loosely.

SLEEVES
Using smaller needles, cast on 20 (20, 24, 24, 28, 28) sts. Place marker and join to work in the round. Work Rib Pattern for 6 (6, 8, 10, 12, 12) rounds.
Change to larger needles and Main Pattern Stitch.
Rounds 1 to 3: Patt.
Round 4: Work 1 st in patt, m1, patt until 1 st rems, m1, patt final st.
Repeat these four rounds 8 (10, 10, 12, 10, 12) times. 36 (40, 44, 48, 48, 52) sts. Work in patt until work measures 8½ (10½, 11½, 12½, 13½, 15)" from cast-on edge, RM.

Sleeve Cap (Worked flat)
Rows 1 and 2: Cast off 2 (2, 3, 3, 3, 3) sts, patt to end of row.
Rows 3 and 4: Cast off 1 (2, 2, 2, 2, 3) sts, patt to end of row.
Rows 5 and 6: Cast off 1 (1, 1, 1, 2, 2) sts, patt to end of row.
Rows 7 and 8: Cast off 0 (0, 0, 0, 1, 1) st, patt to end of row.
Row 9: Ssk, patt until 2 sts remain, 2tog. Work 1 (1, 1, 1, 3, 3) rows in patt
Repeat the last 2 (2, 2, 2, 4, 4) rows 2 (3, 4, 4, 3, 4) times more. 22 (22, 22, 24, 24, 24) sts

Next two rows: Cast off 2 sts, patt to end of row.
Next two rows: Cast off 4 sts, patt to end of row.
Cast off remaining sts.

FINISHING
Sew in sleeves. Weave in all ends.
Wash and dry flat, pulling to shape.

Techniques

MAKING A FRINGE

Cut lengths of yarn by wrapping round a suitably sized book and cutting along one edge. Find a suitable crochet hook - the exact size does not matter. Fold one or two strands in half, forming a loop. You will hold the cut ends together.

Remove the hook, and put the ends of the yarn through the loop.

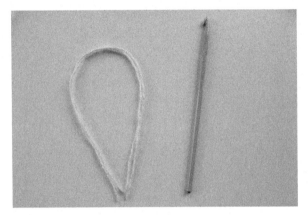

Insert the crochet hook through the place where the fringe is to be. (Here it is in every other cast off stitch of a scarf, and two strands of yarn are used.) Catch the yarn loop on the hook and pull a loop of yarn through.

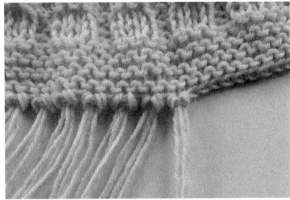

Pull tight, using your fingers to guide the knot into the right place.

Place the tails of yarn over the hook and draw them through the loop of yarn.

Note that on one side you end up with a row of loops over the strands, and on the other just the strands are visible.

MAKING TASSELS

Cut a piece of card about 6" (15 cm) long, or length required, or use a book. Wind the yarn round it, being careful not to wind too tightly. (This stretches the yarn and you end up with a shorter tassel.) Start and stop the yarn at the bottom of the card. Aim for a tassel about the thickness of your finger.

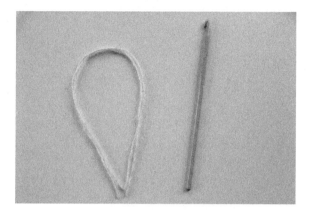

Cut a length of yarn about 2" (60 cm) long, and thread it into a blunt needle. Wind this round the yarn at the top of the card, leaving the free end about the same length as the card. Pull the yarn tight and knot it.

Cut the wound yarn at the bottom of the card. Then smooth the threads down.

Wrap the yarn 3 times then tie tightly. Thread the needle back up through to the top of the tassel and take a stitch round the knot.

Use your fingers to shape the tassel,

then cut the threads evenly. Use the long thread at the top to attached the tassel to its final position.

Tassel making is an art in itself. Feel free to substitute fancier tassels as preferred.

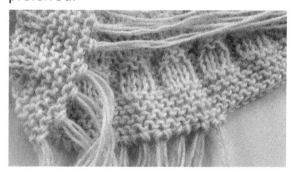

MAKING POMPOMS

These days there are many cheap and efficient pompom makers on the market. If you have one of these, follow the maker's instructions.

In an emergency you can use the old fashioned method of cardboard. Cut two circles of card about the same size as the pompom you want. Cut a smaller circle, about one third of the diameter of the large one, from the centre of each. Thread a tapestry needle or bodkin with the yarn. Hold the two circles together and wrap them with the yarn, until the central hole is almost full. Cut round the edge, separate the card circles slightly and tie yarn very tightly round the centre. Remove the circles and trim the pompom.

PREPARING ROVING FOR KNITTING

Before you start knitting, the roving needs to be opened up and evened out. To do this, hold the end of the roving in one hand, and put your other hand about 10 cm (4") further along. Now pull gently and the fibre will draw apart.

Move both hands about 2.5 cm (1") further along and repeat. You are aiming to increase the length by about 10%.

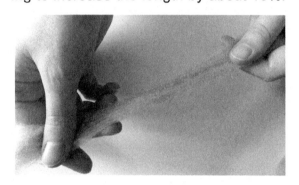

FELTING A BAG

For a felted bag, put bubble wrap inside the bag and between the handles, then place the bag inside a laundry bag or pillow case. Machine wash on a normal 40 degree cycle (not the wool wash) with a low spin. As soon as the cycle has finished, remove the bag and pull into shape. If the bag is not felted to your requirements, repeat the process. Remove the bubble wrap and allow to dry naturally.

LINING A BAG

Felted and unfelted bags can be lined with fabric. Place the dry bag on a piece of paper, and draw round it, outlining the shape and position of the handles for the Project Bag and adding the front of the Kindle Bag. Make a pattern from the paper, adding 1 cm seam allowance, and finishing the lining at the bottom of the garter stitch section for the Project Bag. Sew the body of the lining, then hem into place along the edges.

WORKING I-CORD

Using two cable needles or short double pointed needles, knit the 4 stitches as usual. At the end of the row, do not turn, but slip the sts to the other end of the needle.

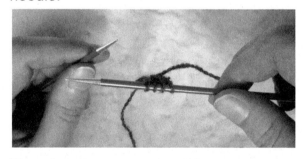

Then knit the next row, pulling the yarn quite tightly for the first stitch, as it is coming from the other end of the row.

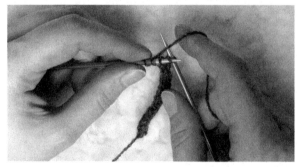

Continue in this way for the length of cord you need. Finish by breaking the yarn, and threading it through the stitches. Fasten off securely on the inside of the cord.

Measurements and Sizing

There is no one way to please every-one! This book will be going all over the world, and 'official' sizes vary hugely in different countries. I have therefore deliberately NOT used clothes sizes (10, 14, 26 etc) nor S, M XL etc, as those terms mean different things to different people.

At the same time, there is the Imperial/metric divide over grams and ounces, inches and centimetres. I personally find it confusing to have both inches and centimetres in the pattern itself, and I have therefore stuck with inches, the units used by the majority of knitters round the world. I find a double sided tape with inches on one side and centi-metres on the other invaluable!

For garments I give both the probably bust/chest size the garment will fit, along with the actual bust/chest size of the garment. If you want a tighter fit, go for a smaller size; if you like a looser fit, go for a bigger size. Garments have been designed to be easy to lengthen or shorten, and to change the length of the sleeves.

Children's garments are particularly difficult to size. Chest size is the best indication, but make sure you knit the sleeves and body long enough for growing room! International standards are similar for children's sizes, so we have used those for the ages on each size.

Using Other Yarns for the Patterns

Although these patterns have been knitted in North Ronaldsay yarn they can easily be used with many other yarns.

BUT YOU MUST SWATCH FOR FIT!

In general, patterns for the 'fine' yarn can be used with most 4 ply/fingering yarns. At 300 m per 100 g, it is fractionally thicker than 4 ply, and sports yarns can also be used. 4 ply sock yarn can work well, but beware of some 'sock' yarn, which is 3 ply thickness.

The aran weight yarn is a true aran, and most aran yarns will work well. In the UK there are a number of 'light aran' yarns. These are a bit thinner, and you may have to adjust needle size to get the right fabric. Again, swatching will tell you what you need to know.

HOW TO WORK OUT IF YOU YARN IS SUITABLE

For a scarf or shawl, where the exact size is not crucial, you can get away with just a small swatch to check you like the fabric. If your tension is looser than given, be aware that you will need more yarn.

Hats and mitts are all very stretchy, so exact size is not crucial. These items are quick to knit, so even if they don't fit the intended victim, they will fit someone.

And as I have said before, Christmas is always coming, and charities are always needing such items.

For a sweater which needs to fit, you will need to go through the following process.

1. Knit a swatch of at least 6" square in the pattern for the given tension. Wash and block it and let it dry. Now measure your tension over 4" and compare it to that given in the pattern. Remember that a small amount off over 4" is 10 times that amount over 40".

2. Look at your finished, washed swatch and decide whether you like the fabric. Is it too tight, too loose, or just right?

3. If your yarn is not a solid colour, check that you like the way the colour and pattern interact.

4. Look at your answers to 1, 2 and 3. If you like the fabric and the tension is spot on, you are ready to go. If not, you need to decide whether to change the needles, or whether to work a size up or down as needed.

5. If you change the CHEST size, you can still use the LENGTHS of your actual body size. Just sit and think it out, with paper and pencil, and away you go! These patterns have been written with minimal shaping to allow for such changes.

Variations

Most of the patterns in this book can be easily adapted.
Here are some suggestions: it is not an exhaustive list!

PAGE 12 TRIANGULAR SHAWL

The edging can be omitted, or changed to another pattern. You can easily add up to about 10 stitches each side, and 5 at the tip, without changing the overall look. The centre can be made as large as you like, just finish after a completed 'paw', then knit a few rows before casting off loosely. The shawl can also be knitted in other weights of yarn, from cobweb to chunky!

PAGE 14 GARTER RIB COLLAR

The size of this can easily be changed by adding multiples of 2 stitches. Make it long for a scarf.

PAGE 15 BETTY MARTIN COWL

A cowl with a bigger circumference (for example, to wind twice round the neck) can be made by adding multiples of 4 stitches, or try doubling the number of stitches for the size you want. The height of the cowl can be increased or decreased.

For a **headband**, cast on the same number of stitches but only work 2 or 3" before casting off. Many other textured stitch patterns can be used for this cowl. In particular, the cowl can be made to match the Mistake Ribbing mitts and the Garter Rib mitts (p18). The garter rib pattern fits the cowl pattern exactly, but the mistake ribbing needs an odd number of stitches, so cast on 1 more stitch.

PAGE 16 MISTAKE RIB BEANIE

This stitch pattern is very stretchy. Make it tighter to the head by working a shorter piece before starting the shaping at the crown. Or make it longer by working more. Tassels and bobbles can look good on this one!

PAGE 18 FINGERLESS MITTENS

These are so quick and easy to make and adapt! Make the cuff longer or shorter. Make then in different yarns.

PAGE 20 SWITHA CUSHION

The stitch pattern can be changed easily. Betty Martin has roughly the same stitch tension as stocking stitch, so many knit/purl patterns can be used. If preferred, the two sides can be knitted the same, and the pad can be sewn or crocheted in. Or a zip can be used.

PAGE 22 FLOTTA CUSHION

The Flotta cushion can be made up with the same back as the Switha Cushion. Or alter the gansey motifs in the panels.

PAGE 24 CAT'S PAW WRAP

Many lace stitch patterns can be used for the centre of this wrap. A few more stitches can be added to the width, or taken away, without altering the size too much. It can be made longer or shorter, wider or narrower. Use this pattern as a template and add your own favourite stitch patterns!

PAGE 26 SIMPLE LACY SWEATERS

These boat necked sweaters can be altered in many ways. Different stitch patterns can be used, and the body length can be varied from super cropped to low hip length. Similarly the sleeves can be long, mid or short.

PAGE 28 LACY SCARVES

The width of the scarf can be changed by adding or subtracting one stitch pattern repeat, and the scarf can be made any length. Any other stitch pattern can used, and the scarves can be worked in stocking stitch with a garter stitch border if preferred. They can also be worked in almost any yarn thickness, from cobweb to chunky.

PAGE 30 LACY COWLS

Any sized cowl can be made by adding or subtracting stitch pattern repeats. A cowl to wind twice round the neck can be made by doubling the number of stitches for the size you want. The height of the cowl can be increased or decreased.

PAGE 32 LACY CUSHIONS

It is possible to make a cushion using different stitches for the front and back. Cushions can also be made in one piece, with 9 rows of garter stitch at the beginning and end, to make a cushion back like the aran weight ones (p20). Remember that to make the cushion look plump, and to make the pattern stand out, the cover needs to be smaller than the pad. The patterns can easily be adapted for other sizes of cushion pad, and other stitch patterns can be used in the same way.

PAGE 35 CAT'S PAW STRIPE SCARF

This can be made wider (it would make a good wrap!) by adding multiples of 11 stitches. It can also be made longer or shorter, and in many weights of yarn.

PAGE 36 SAMPLER THROW

The throw can be made any size, to fit armchair to double bed, and can also be used as a shawl or a knee rug. Just knit more squares. A crochet border can be used instead of the Old Shale border. It can be worked in thicker yarn, using the same colour yarn throughout, or using different colours. Individual squares can be made up into cushions.

PAGE 42 STOCKING STITCH TOP

Note that these changes all require more yarn.

High Low Hem: Work the Back for 2 or 3" longer before changing to stocking stitch.

Tunic length: Work back and front to 19" or the required length before starting the armhole shaping.

Ribbed hem: For back and front, cast on required number of stitches loosely using 3.75 mm needles. Work either 1 to 3" in k1, p1 rib. Change to 5 mm needles and work in stocking stitch until the work measures 16" or the required length before starting the armhole shaping.

PAGE 45 END-TO-END CRESCENT

This can be made longer or shorter by adjusting the number of central repeats worked before decreasing.
It also works well in other thicknesses of yarn.

PAGE 50 BERET AND FINGERLESS MITTENS

For a short 'stalk' on the top of the beret work 1" i-cord only.

If preferred, the i-cord can be omitted. Draw the yarn through the remaining stitches an sew the seam. A pompom, wool or fur, large or small, can be added instead.

Note that I have used a different colour yarn for the ribbing of the beret and mittens. This was because I was not sure whether I had enough of the variegated yarn! You could do the same, or work them all in the same yarn.

PAGE 52 ROVING BAGS

Elly's Big Balls of roving can be spun, but they can also be used directly. You will need to thin the roving out a bit (p100) I give patterns for bags made with one and two balls, but many other sizes can be made in the same way. They bags can also be felted and/or lined (p100). Cushions, cowls and hats can be made in the same way.

PAGE 54 V-NECKED VEST

This unisex vest can be knitted to any length by adjusting the length before the start of the armholes and neck. The stitch patterns can be altered, repeated or omitted as desired. The pattern will also work in stocking stitch to show off a colourful yarn.

PAGE 58 BRAELAND SWEATER
PAGE 60 QUOYEDEN SWEATER
PAGE 64 BLANSTER SWEATER

These three sweaters can all be altered in the same way to make tunics, and to have different necks.

For a tunic: Omit the ribbing and instead work 1 to 1½" garter stitch on the smaller needles at the bottom of the hem and cuffs.

For a cropped jersey: Work as for the tunic, but to the desired length.

Stand Up Neck: Graft shoulders and pick up stitches on the smaller needles as for crew neck. Work 10 rounds in garter stitch (k one round, p the next). Cast off loosely.

Bagel Neck: Graft shoulders and pick up stitches on the smaller needle as for crew neck. Work 10 rounds in garter stitch (k one round, p the next). Change to larger needles and knit 10 rounds. Cast off loosely.

Roll Neck: Graft shoulders and pick up stitches on the smaller needles as for crew neck. Work about 2" in k1, p1 rib. Change to the larger needle and work a further 2 - 3".

PAGE 68 BRAELAND HAT

This can be changed into a beanie by working 5 or 6 rows of rib at the start, It can also be made slouchy by working longer before the crown shaping, and a bobble or tassel can be added.

PAGE 70 QUOYEDEN HAT

This can be changed like the Braeland hat. Other stitch patterns from the sweater can be used instead of what is charted. Just make sure the total number of rows is about the same.

PAGE 72 BLANSTER HAT

This can be changed to a ribbed brim. Omit the brim and work the same number of rows in k1, p2 rib instead. The hat can be made deeper by adding a few rows of pattern before starting the crown shaping.

PAGE 74 BRAELAND MITTENS
PAGE 76 QUOYEDEN AND
BLANSTER MITTENS
All mitten designs can have longer or
shorter cuffs, and the palm and fingers
can be made longer or shorter. For
fingerless mittens work a coupe of plain
and a couple of ribbing rows on the
thumb before casting off. Work the palm
to just short of the length you want, then
add a few rows of ribbing and casting off.

PAGE 78 BRAELAND, QUOYEDEN
AND BLANSTER SCARVES
All scarves can be made wider by adding
stitch repeats. They can also be made
any length. They also work well in DK
yarns.

PAGE 80 CAT'S PAW CROPPED TOP
I have here made it into a cropped top,
but the piece can be made any length by
increasing the number of stitch repeats
before and after the neck shaping. The
front and back can be the same length,
or different, and a belt could be made to
cinch it at the waist or hips. Extra stitch
repeats will make a wider top, to cover
more of your arms. And you can change
the stitch pattern to you favourite lacy
motif.

PAGE 82 CABLED SCARF
This one was made with men in mind, but
it is unisex! Make is wider or narrower by
adding or subtracting the stitch repeat,
and make it as long as you like. This is
another piece which also works very well
in DK yarn.

PAGE 84 CHILD'S VEST
I have made this with plenty of length, but
of your child likes a shorter piece, then
work less before shaping the armholes.
You can also change the stitch motif.

PAGE 86 STRIPED TRIANGULAR
SHAWL
The shawl can be made smaller or larger
by cganging the number of rows worked.
It can also be worked in one colour.

PAGE 91 FLOUER SHAWL
For a larger shawl keep repeating the 12
rows of the main pattern before working
the top edge.

PAGE 95 FAIRNTECKLE
CHILDREN'S SWEATER
If preferred this can be worked in stocking
stitch.

Patterns by Type and Yarn Weight

(A) is an aran weight pattern and (F) is a 4 ply/fingering pattern.

SHAWLS AND WRAPS

Cat's Paw Triangular Shawl (F) 12
Cat's Paw Wrap (F) 24
End-To-End Crescent (F) 45
Flouer Shawl (F) 91
Striped Triangular Shawl (F) 86
Skinny Crescent Shawl (F) 88

HATS

Beret (F) 50
Blanster Hat (A) 72
Braeland Hat (A) 68
Mistake Rib Beanie (A) 16
Quoyeden Hat (A) 70

MITTENS

Betty Martin Fingerless Mittens (A) 18
Blanster Mittens (A) 76
Braeland Mittens (A) 74
Garter Rib Fingerless Mittens (A) 18
Mistake Rib Fingerless Mittens (A) 18
Quoyeden Mittens (A) 76
Stocking Stitch Fingerless Mittens (F) 50

COWLS

Betty Martin Cowl (A) 15
Garter Rib Collar (A) 14
Horseshoe Cowl (F) 30
Miniature Leaf Cowl (F) 30
New Shell Cowl (F) 30

SCARVES

Blanster Scarf (A) 78
Braeland Scarf (A) 78
Cabled Scarf (A) 82
Cat's Paw Stripe Scarf (F) 35
Horseshoe Scarf (F) 28
Miniature Leaf Scarf (F) 28
New Shell Scarf (F) 28
Quoyeden Scarf (A) 78

SWEATERS

Blanster Sweater (A) 64
Braeland Sweater (A) 58
Cat's Paw Cropped Top (F) 80
Fairnteckle Child's Sweater (A) 95
Miniature Leaf Sweater (F) 26
Quoyeden Sweater (A) 60
Razor Shell Sweater (F) 26
Stocking Stitch Top (F) 42

VESTS

Child's Vest (F) 84
V necked Vest (A) 34

HOMEWARES

Cat's Paw Stripe Cushion (F) 32
Fircone Cushion (F) 32
Flotta Cushion (A) 22
Roving Bags 52
Sampler Throw (F) 36
Shetland Eyelet Cushion (F) 32
Switha Cushion (A) 20

Pattern Notes, Abbreviations and Chart Symbols

Please read these before you start any pattern:
any queries may well be answered here!

GENERAL NOTES

The colour of both the natural North Ronaldsay and the hand dyed yarn varies from batch to batch. Yarn amounts are always approximate. If you substitute yarns the yardage may vary. Again, make sure you buy enough to complete your project.

Projects knitted in the round are suitable for 4 or 5 dpns or circular needles. The choice is yours!

The size or age of the 'to fit' is an approximate based on the amount of ease most folk like. Please refer to the actual size of the garment if you want a different fit.

If your tension is not right change the needle size. NEVER try to knit more tightly or more loosely - it doesn't work!

PATTERN NOTES

If only one number is given, it is for all sizes.

After casting off, the stitch left on the needle is included in the stitch count after the cast off.

The markèrs are not mentioned unless they are important. Slip markers as you get to them.

GENERAL ABBREVIATIONS

alt	alternate
approx	approximately
beg	beginning
CC	contrasting colour
cont	continue
dec	decrease
dpn(s)	double pointed needle(s)
inc	increase/increasing
LH	left hand
M	marker
MC	main colour
PM	place marker
rnd(s)	round(s)
RH	right hand
RSF	right side facing
SM	slip marker
st(s)	stitch(es)
tog	together
WS	wrong side
W&T	wrap and turn

WORKING FROM A CHART

Each square on the chart represents one stitch or action. Charts are read from the bottom up.

When working to and fro, odd numbered rows are read from right to left, and even numbered rows from left to right.

When working in the round, every row is read from right to left.

KEY TO CHART SYMBOLS

Key

RS: knit
WS: purl

• RS: purl
WS: knit

no stitch

O yo

$ s1p

/ RS: k2tog
WS: p2tog

\ RS: ssk
WS: p2togtbl

▲ k3togtbl

⌒ cast off

← move marker 1 stitch left

→ move marker 1 stitch right

C4B

position of marker

stitch repeat

Ω k1tbl

Charts have been made using Stitch Mastery by Cathy Scott, available at www.stitchmastery.com

KNITTING ABBREVIATIONS

C4B	place the next 4 sts onto the cable needle and hold at the back of the work, k2, k2 from the cable needle
k	knit
kfb	knit into front and back of stitch
kfbf	knit into front, back and front of stitch
k2tog	knit the next two sts together
k3tog	knit the next three sts together
kwise	knitwise
m1	make 1 by picking up the strand before the next st and knitting into the back of it
m1p	make 1 purlwise
p	purl
p2tog	purl 2 together
pfb	purl into front and back of stitch
psso	pass slipped st over
pwise	purlwise
s1	slip 1 stitch
s1p	slip 1 stitch purlwise
ssk	slip 2 sts (one at a time), knit 2 slipped stitches together tbl
tbl	through back loop
W&T	yarn forward, slip the next stitch, yarn back, return the slipped stitch to other needle
yo	yarn over

My thanks go to all the models for their patience - Elly Doyle, Nick Lovick, Rachael Murton, Claire Omand, Sue Robinson, Natasha Stacey, Jill Strutt and Daniel Vincent.

Photographs from the original book are by Nick Lovick.

Index

abbreviations 108

bag 52
beanie 16
Beret 50
Betty Martin Fingerless Mittens 18
Blanster Hat 72
Blanster Mittens 76
Blanster Scarf 78
Blanster Sweater 64
blocking/dressing 11
Braeland Mittens 74
Braeland Hat 68
Braeland Scarf 78
Braeland Sweater 58

Cabled Scarf 82
care of pieces 10
Cat's Paw Cropped Top 80
Cat's Paw Stripe Cushion 32
Cat's Paw Stripe Scarf 35
Cat's Paw Triangular Shawl 12
Cat's Paw Wrap 24
chart symbols 108
children
    Beret 50
    Betty Martin Cowl 15
    Betty Martin Fingerless Mittens 18
    Blanster Hat 72
    Braeland Mittens 74
    Blanster Scarf 78
    Braeland Hat 68
    Blanster Mittens 76
    Braeland Scarf 78
    Fairnteckle Sweater 95
    Garter Rib Collar 14
    Garter Rib Fingerless Mittens 18
    Horseshoe Cowl 30
    Horseshoe Scarf 28
    Miniature Leaf Cowl 30
    Miniature Leaf Scarf 28
    Mistake Rib Beanie 16
    Mistake Rib Fingerless Mittens 18
    New Shell Cowl 30
    New Shell Scarf 28
    Quoyeden Hat 70
    Quoyeden Mittens 76
    Quoyeden Scarf 78
    Stocking Stitch Fingerless Mittens .. 50
    Vest 84
Child's Vest 84
collar 14
cowl
    Betty Martin Cowl 15
    Horseshoe Cowl 30
    Miniature Leaf Cowl 30
    New Shell Cowl 30
crescent shawl
    end-to-end 45
    Skinny Crescent Shawl 88
cushion
    Cat's Paw Stripe Cushion 32
    Fircone Cushion 32
    Flotta Cushion 22
    Shetland Eyelet Cushion 32
    Switha Cushion 20

dressing/blocking 11

End-To-End Crescent 45

Fairnteckle Child's Sweater 95
fingerless mittens
    Betty Martin Fingerless Mittens 18
    Garter Rib Fingerless Mittens 18
    Mistake Rib Fingerless Mittens 18
    Stocking Stitch Fingerless Mittens .. 50
Fircone Cushion 32
Flotta Cushion 22
Flouer Shawl 91

Garter Rib Collar 14
Garter Rib Fingerless Mittens 18

hat
     Beret 50
     Blanster Hat 72
     Braeland Hat 68
     Mistake Rib Beanie 16
     Quoyeden Hat 70
Horseshoe Cowl 30
Horseshoe Scarf 28

introduction 3

measurements 101
Miniature Leaf Cowl 30
Miniature Leaf Scarf 28
Miniature Leaf Sweater 26
Mistake Rib Beanie 16
Mistake Rib Fingerless Mittens 18
mittens
     Braeland Mittens 74
     Blanster Mittens 76
     Quoyeden Mittens 76

New Shell Cowl 30
New Shell Scarf 28
North Ronaldsay sheep 6
North Ronaldsay yarn 8

patterns by type 107
pattern note 108

Quoyeden Hat 70
Quoyeden Mittens 76
Quoyeden Scarf 78
Quoyeden Sweater 60

Razor Shell Sweater 26
Roving Bags 52

Sampler Throw 36
scarf
     Blanster Scarf 78
     Braeland Scarf 78
     Cabled Scarf 82
     Cat's Paw Stripe Scarf 35

Horseshoe Scarf 28
Miniature Leaf Scarf 28
New Shell Scarf 28
Quoyeden Scarf 78
shawl
     Cat's Paw Triangular Shawl 12
     Cat's Paw Wrap 24
     End-To-End Crescent 45
     Flouer Shawl 91
     Skinny Crescent Shawl 88
     Striped Triangular Shawl 86
Shetland Eyelet Cushion 32
sizing 101
Skinny Crescent Shawl 88
Stocking Stitch Fingerless Mittens 50
Stocking Stitch Top 42
Striped Triangular Shawl 86
swatching 11
sweater
     Blanster Sweater 64
     Braeland Sweater 58
     Cat's Paw Cropped Top 80
     Fairnteckle Child's Sweater 95
     Miniature Leaf Sweater 26
     Quoyeden Sweater 60
     Razor Shell Sweater 26
     Stocking Stitch Top 42
Switha Cushion 20

techniques
     felting a bag 100
     fringe 98
     lining a bag 100
     making pompoms 99
     making tassels 99
     preparing roving 100
     working i-cord 100

using other yarns 102

V necked Vest 34
variations 103
vest
     V necked Vest 34
     Child's Vest 84

washing wool pieces 10

CPSIA information can be obtained
at www.ICGtesting.com
Printed in the USA
BVOW05s1419210917
495457BV00027B/1034/P